Writing With Purpose
A Step-by-Step Guide to Producing Your Best Book

by W.A. Fulkerson

First Edition, April 2016

Cover Art by MNS Art Studio

Published by Perennial Press

This book was printed and distributed in conjunction with Perennial Press. First published in the United States of America

For news and updates on upcoming novels by W.A. Fulkerson, visit www.wafulkerson.com and sign up for the mailing list.

ISBN: 978 0 692 68794 9

Other Books by W.A. Fulkerson:

The Starfall Trilogy
Starfall
Star-Crossed
Starborn

Short Story Collections
A Noticeable Limp

Coming Soon
The Weathermen (Winter 2016)
For Whom the Sun Sings (2017)

Praise For *Writing With Purpose:*

"Smart like a professor and encouraging like an old friend, *Writing With Purpose* does for novelists what *Save The Cat* did for screenwriters. The kind of book that somehow makes you better without destroying your morale. A warm, witty, and wonderful read."

- Brian Ivie, Award-Winning Writer/Director of "The Drop Box"

"Sparkling prose and good advice spiced with compelling examples. Fulkerson not only teaches us something essential about writing -- and ourselves-- but makes us have fun learning it. Wisdom doesn't have to be hard to swallow. Who knew?"

– David D. Esselstrom, Ph.D. Professor and Chair of the English Department, Azusa Pacific University

"I get asked to do a lot of book reviews, but every now and then I get the privilege of reading a book from someone who really knows how to put words on paper... a true *author.* Wesley Fulkerson is one of those people. He has a gift for writing, and throughout his book he explains how you can become a better writer yourself. It has already helped me (the information of purpose alone is reason enough to read this) and I'm sure you will get a lot out of your time spent with this great book. Enjoy!"

- Henry J. Evans, Author of the Amazon Bestselling Hour a Day Entrepreneur

"*Writing With Purpose* expands the boundaries of traditional writing guides, tremendously useful to the new author as well the expert. Beyond plot, character, and world-building, it explores the psychology, research, and all-encompassing purpose necessary to crafting a first-class novel. Readers are prodded not only to ponder what they want to write about, but *why* they want to write it, making all the difference in their own creations. Be warned: the mix of instructional, inspirational, insightful, and comedic narrative makes this guide tremendously hard to put down, and once the cover closes, you'll find yourself reaching for a pen!"

– Levi Stack, Author of <u>The Silent Deal</u>, <u>The Magic Trick</u>

Praise For *Starfall*:

"Very epic and highly addictive!" – **YA Book Review**

"I couldn't put the book down, but when I did I couldn't wait to pick it back up!" – **Vivacious Fiction**

"...this take on the genre is so incredibly unique! The world-building was phenomenal, and the attention to detail very rewarding. I could watch the book like a movie in my head." – **GreenRoomBooks**

"*Starfall* is a fantastic fantasy novel." – **BenjaminOfTomes**

Table of Contents:

Part I: Getting It Done

1. **This Pun Was on Porpoise-**
    laying a foundation for your work   *11*

2. **Dr. Know-**
    preparing to create   *25*

3. **Follow That Character!**
    populating your literary world   *37*

4. **Ender's Ending-**
    where's this thing headed?   *53*

5. **Writers Write and Writer's Block-**
    getting things done and overcoming obstacles *65*

6. **Touching Up the Corners-**
    the editing process and refining your work   *83*

Part II: Honing Your Craft

7. **Adventure is Out There!**
    ...and you're still in here?   *99*

8. **Psycho-**
    understanding how people work   *109*

9. Framing Your Vision-
creating the world in which you write   *123*

10. Speako dee Englush?
Fluency and the tools of the trade   *133*

11.Breathing In-
learning to be inspired constantly   *147*

12.The Tremendous Responsibility
of the Artist   *159*

Acknowledgements   *166*

Notes   *167*

Introduction:
Why This Book?

It's a fair question. Aren't there infinite books out there on the subject of writing, honing your craft, and tools for success? In a word, yes, and that is the problem to which this book is the answer. Sound confusing? Bear with me.

There are countless books on writing and creative disciplines- many of them even offer valuable insights. The problem I have found with such manuals, however, is that none of them are comprehensive, and they seem to lack a cohesive, underlying philosophy. One book, such as *The Creative Habit* by Twyla Tharp (an excellent read), will give you ideas for how to get more done each day. Another, such as *Writing the Breakout Novel* by Donald Maas, will give you tips and tricks for refining the novel you're already working on. Others offer ideas on how to practice writing or come up with new ideas, how to live an inspired life, etcetera. There are a myriad of books to wade through and an ocean of information.

This book serves as an island, or if I may be so bold, the New World. It is the simplicity on the far side of complexity. Having waded through a number of these tomes myself, as well as having spent years writing novels, working as head writer for Arbella Studios, and consulting on various writing projects over time, I see a coherent philosophy that ties it all together.

You don't want to read fifty books on writing (unless you're a sadist). You want to read one book. It is my intention for this volume to be that one book and to save you a great deal of time.

This book is for you if you have always wanted to write but can't ever seem to finish anything. This book is for you if you are a historically prolific writer lately feeling dry and uninspired. If you are new to writing and looking to improve your skills, if you aren't a writer but you enjoy reading and you want to better understand the mind of the author, if you are writing fiction, nonfiction, comic books, philosophy, or poetry, this book is for you.

Whatever brings you here to this page, I am excited for you and your journey. I intend to serve as your guide, warning you of pitfalls and hidden dangers, building you up to surpass your limitations, and to instruct you step by step on how to succeed. You might be in the trenches, but so am I, and I've got your back. I am with you in this.

This book is divided up into two parts. Part I deals with the actual writing process and how to go about writing in a better way. Part II is focused on honing your craft as a writer and improving daily, so that every book is better than the last. At the end of each chapter are action items or exercises. I strongly encourage you to do them. I know that it's the part of the book you would normally skim over or skip entirely, but I promise that actually taking the time to use this book like a workbook will ensure that you get the most out of your time.

Through it all I trust that you will find a compelling and coherent philosophy of writing. What is that philosophy, you may ask?

Read on...

-W.A. Fulkerson
October 8, 2015

Part I:

Getting It Done

Chapter One: This Pun Was on Porpoise
laying a foundation for your work

Aaand we start the book with a groan. Where is my editor?

I'm kidding, of course. I know where my editor is. He's in Hawaii, spending my money. At any rate, I promise that there is a reason for the cheesy chapter name.

A month or so back I read a book by the illustrious author, Anne McCaffrey. For those of you unfamiliar with her work, McCaffrey is a paragon in the fantasy genre, creating an entirely new way of thinking among writers of fantasy literature. Her novels taking place in the beloved world of Pern have captured the hearts of readers for decades, and some, including *Dragonflight* and *Dragonquest*, have even garnered praise from staunch critics. She has inspired an entire generation of fantasy writers with her ideas of symbiosis between dragon and man, defining and heralding the 'dragonrider' sub-genre of fantasy. The book of hers I most recently read was called *The Dolphins of Pern*.

I don't think it was her best work.

It wasn't anything blatant. There were some interesting ideas. McCaffrey knows how to come up with characters and interesting situations. And yet it was the sort of book that you finish, set down on your night stand, and say, "K." It didn't captivate me.

I hope the die-hard McCaffrey fans out there haven't grabbed their torches and pitchforks yet, or at least that they haven't figured out where I live. McCaffrey is a good writer and her reputation is in no danger from me. Yet *The Dolphins of Pern* illustrates a common pitfall in writing and it is beneficial for us to examine it. Why isn't it as captivating as *Dragonflight* or *Dragonquest*?

The novel didn't have a clear purpose, and every page of the story lamented that fact.

Do you forgive me for the pun now?

What Drives a Story?

Do you ever finish a book and at the end wonder, "What was the point of that?" I know I certainly do. Writing without a purpose is a problem nearly ubiquitous among inexperienced writers, and it is even occasional among the best and most seasoned of authors. It's nothing to be ashamed of; it's something to be corrected, an opportunity for growth. We're going to cover a lot of ground in this book, but if you take one single thing away, remember this: *write with a purpose.*

Everything in the real world has a purpose, even if you don't always get to see what it is. If your book doesn't come from a place of deep purpose, your readers will sense it and it will seem like the fiction that it is; whether you're writing high fantasy about elves and ogres or an agricultural treatise on potato-farming. If you don't know why you're writing, I sure as heck am not going to know why I'm reading.

In my experience, you don't want your readers wondering why they're reading your book.

Anything Can Be Your Purpose

Should the nice guy always get the girl? Write about it. Does crime never pay? Write about it. Should potato farmers in the southeastern quadrant of Idaho be using soil with a higher rating of nitrate-density for most of their fields? Put a cork in it. No one wants to hear about that. (Kidding.)

McCaffrey's book was not all that it could be, in a large degree because it felt like she went to the aquarium, learned a bunch of fun facts about dolphins, and wrote a story with a lot of dolphins in it. "I want to write about dolphins" may be inspiration, but it certainly isn't a purpose, and if your porpoise has no purpose, then your poor, poised for disappointment story will purpose you for the recently repurposed poor house. (I really hope my editor gets back soon...) *The Dolphins of Pern* had a lot of potential that it failed to realize, but very easily could have if it was a purpose-driven novel. The novel could have been written with any number of strong purposes energizing it, such as "The call to adventure should be heeded above all else," or "A father's greatest responsibility is making his son a better man than he ever was," or "The earth is our home and we need to take care of it." Everything else falls into place once you have a purpose. So we want to write a book with dolphins in it. Great. Any one of those purposes and a myriad of others can be used in a story with dolphins.

Purpose is the battery pack that makes a story go. It is the goal you are working towards, the sermon you are preaching, the refrain in the melody that you sing. A book without a well-defined purpose is pretty worthless. It's a speedboat without a propeller.

Every worthwhile book that has ever been written has a moral, like it or not. *Slaughterhouse Five* fits the bill. So does *Lord of the Rings, Capitalism and Freedom,* the *Communist Manifesto, The Scarlet Letter, Harry Potter,* and *The Road.* These books aren't similar, notice. Some great books even have such a dark purpose that we would never pretend to call it a lesson in ethics.

Nonetheless, every great book has a moral. Whether you agree with the moral or not is irrelevant at the moment. Every great book has a purpose behind the writing from which the author wrote.

A Word of Caution

If the purpose behind your book is, for example, "It always pays to do the right thing," your book should not look anything even close to the following:

> *"Hey, Greg. You had a tough decision there, but it always pays to do the right thing."*
> *"It sure does, Hank. It wasn't easy, but like you said, it always pays to do the right thing."*
> *"Amen, amen. You know what, Greg? I'm going to actually pay you because doing the right thing pays. Here's forty, sixty, eighty..."*

NO. Bad dog. NO.

Writing with clear purpose does not mean being blindingly obvious at every turn. There is such a thing as subtlety, and please- use it. "Show don't tell" really is a pretty decent rule of thumb when you're trying to figure out how to get a point across. So is controversy! Don't make it too easy for your characters. There should be moments of doubt because there are moments of doubt in life. This will make your story relatable.

It is imperative that you as the author know exactly what your purpose is, not that you put it in quotations on every single page. Some of the scripts

I've read, let me tell you... *shakes head*

Some Excellent Examples of Purpose-Driven Storytelling

C.S. Lewis, one of my all-time favorite authors, once wrote a fascinating book entitled *A Grief Observed*. He wrote it with the intention of chronicling and sharing his mourning process after his wife tragically died of cancer. In the book you see Lewis, a great man of faith, an intellectual giant for whom no question seems too hard or great enough to shake him, appearing broken, doubting, weak. Having dedicated his life to God, he finds himself enraged at God. A lifelong romantic and devotee of his beloved wife, he finds himself forgetting what she looked like. No amount of anguish or pain or suffering seems likely to bring her back, and yet this is precisely the path that he walks for so long.

I do not often cry while reading a book, but for this one I wept. I dare say that I don't know a single person who has read it who was not deeply, deeply moved.

C.S. Lewis had a very clear motive in mind as he wrote: transparency. His purpose was to chronicle the truth no matter how difficult, confusing, or damaging. He walked a long, hard road, but he was perhaps stronger by the end. His purpose gave the work meaning and depth as he found his way back to faith, reason, and enduring hope throughout life under the sun.

Mary Shelly's haunting classic *Frankenstein* recounts the travels and travails of Dr. Frankenstein and his notorious monster. Dr. Frankenstein, an intelligent but reclusive student obsessed with the old magics of alchemy and dark arts, decides to consider ancient problems through a modern, scientific lens. His years of frenzied labor end up producing the impossible: animation of a lifeless body. Yet the cursed doctor's greatest triumph is also his undoing, as the monster he created systematically dismantles his life, murdering everyone he cares about. Delving into the darkness proves to be his everlasting regret.

When you finish it, you almost can't help but shudder.

Shelly's purpose is to warn the reader that there are consequences for defying natural law and that there are perhaps some realms of knowledge better left unexplored. This gothic masterpiece's striking imagery and foreboding tone drive the point home all too well. Her purpose is not explicit on every page of course, and yet every thought and every word in *Frankenstein* derives its source from these ideas, from this purpose. It is what gives the story its power.

These examples that I've chosen, one nonfiction, the other a novel, are both works in which it is very easy for the reader to ascertain the writer's purpose. I don't expect much debate from the reader on either example, but for other books people will invariably have lively debates as to what the author's purpose was in writing. Even so, there is no debate that such a book *has* a deep purpose and that the author knows what it is. It is the difference between hearing a native speaker and a foreigner try to speak the same language. The reader always knows the real thing when he sees it. It feels like the real world, and it rings true.

I suppose that at the end of the day, only the writer himself can tell you his purpose for certain, and in many cases the author declines to disclose this information, preferring to allow the work to speak for itself. This is a reasonable sentiment, and one that I personally have a great deal of sympathy for. However, for the sake of this book, I will share with you the purpose that drove a few of the novels that I've written to date. I'll do my best to avoid spoilers for those of you unfamiliar with my fictional works.

Personally...

The first novel I ever wrote was volume one in a trilogy of fantasy novels called *Starfall*. It is an epic adventure that takes place in an unfamiliar world called Pontus, where people are born with stars in the sky that fall to the ground when they least expect, offering them the chance for a gift that will change them entirely. The books follow twin brothers Ducasus and Malleus, first appearing as ungifted slaves watching their stars in the country of Flaroria, where the gifted inhabitants are blessed with super speed. The two brothers are thrown onto two very different and yet parallel paths of adventure, love, loss, turmoil, triumph, and intrigue, leading to a grand conflict that threatens the very existence of Pontus itself.

There is no greater satisfaction for the writer than to know that he has written what he was meant to and that it has touched someone. I have been extremely blessed to have written these books that have moved so many hearts. I hear comments all the time of which characters resonated with particular readers, which gifts they imagine themselves choosing if they had a star, at what points in the story they were angry, elated, laughing, frustrated, and delighted. It warms my heart to hear how people talk about these books.

So what was my purpose in writing them?

In the first place, I wanted to write a different sort of fantasy novel. As a kid I grew up adoring the work of J.R.R. Tolkien, C.S. Lewis, and others. The problem in my mind, however, was that though I loved fantasy literature, it seemed to me that so much of it was derivative of the greats. Most fantasy novels were set either in Tolkien's world (Dwarves, Orcs, and Elves) or in McCaffrey's (farm boys who discover they were meant to ride dragons). I, in my very youthful and audacious inexperience, wanted to write something to reinvigorate the genre. My hope was to create another canvas to be painted on by others down the road. Thus, I set out to create a whole new fantasy- a totally new mythology complete with new mythological creatures and races, a world and a history the likes of which had never been seen before. You as the reader may judge for yourself as to whether or not you feel that I was successful. Hopefully the fullness of my purpose is realized, as only time will tell.

This was an exciting idea, and it helped get me started, but it wasn't a true purpose. I needed to dig deeper, past the façade and into the structure, past the skin and into the heart.

The purpose I discovered was this:

I wanted to get across the idea that all of those countless people out there in the world today who think that they are worthless and don't have an impact are, in fact, of tremendous importance to those around them. Even if they couldn't see it themselves, I wanted to put them in the shoes of a protagonist who feels the same way (Ducasus). By the end we realize that this humble, rather average young man is actually extraordinary, and Pontus never would have survived without him. This was something near and dear to my heart, because growing up I always felt like I was sort of the bland person who didn't really matter all that much. It was a lie, of course, but it took me an awful long time to figure that out. Even as you read these words now, please know that you matter very much to the people God has placed around you. What you do and how you love and how you live matters to the utmost.

This brings me to another point that I will have to elaborate on further in a later chapter- write what you know and what is near and dear to your heart. I mention it now just to say that that is what I did with *Starfall*, and it's been working out pretty well. Why not try the same thing? Find your purpose in that which stirs your heart. More on that later.

It bears mentioning that without the moral purpose of *Starfall*, the book would have suffered from the same deficiency as the dolphin book. Wanting to write something new is a great bit of inspiration and a way to help get something started, but ultimately, without a deeper purpose- an emotional purpose- the book would not have been as good.

In *The Weathermen* I set out to write a sort of modern-day magical realism in which everything was just like it is in the real world except for one major tweak: there are a mysterious group of men and women born with the ability to influence and change the weather. If I had stopped here it would not have been a very good book, because though this was an impetus to writing, I was not ready to start until I knew what my underlying purpose in writing the book would be. I decided on this: Deep in their souls, men think that they are gods, but even in the greatest of individuals this is a tragically laughable notion. I set out to show this through the life and adventures of Jessica, Tony, and April, as well as all of the Weathermen, of course. My purpose drove the story, kept me going when I wasn't sure where to go, and constantly provided ideas for interesting scenes and dialog.

That's enough about me. I'll let my purpose behind writing the others remain a mystery for now, unless any of you out there care to offer me exorbitant amounts of money to know. In that case I'll reconsider my position.

The Purpose of This Book

I am passionate about writing. It's something I was made to do. If you sit me down with a cup of hot vanilla rooibos tea and ask me to talk about the writing process, I could go on for hours. Partially because I love writing, partially because I love talking, but also because I'm really hoping you'll pour me a second cup of tea. (Just my opinion, but vanilla rooibos tea is the best beverage for writing. Give it a try. Live a little.)

It breaks my heart, though, whenever I speak with students in writing classes or when I remember much of my own education in writing. The sad fact of the matter is that it is often taught very poorly in this day and age. There are exceptions, of course, and I had a couple of teachers cross my path who taught me well, but they were very rare. Creative writing in particular is taught very poorly.[1] The reason I'm able to sit here and type away at this manuscript is because I have a purpose in doing so. I want to see better writing in this world, and whatever I can do to help make that happen is well worth it to me.

In a phrase, my purpose behind writing this book is a desire to set the record straight as it pertains to writing, and particularly creative writing. I want to come alongside other writers and aspiring writers to teach what I have been so fortunate to learn as we both journey on to becoming the best writers we can be.

Finding Your Purpose

This seems like a daunting task, perhaps, but if you are willing to do some honest deep-thinking and a little bit of soul-searching, you shouldn't have too much trouble. For some writers, their purpose remains the same throughout every book that they write. I think of the famous Roman senator Cato the Elder who ended every single speech with "Carthago delenda est." (Carthage must be destroyed.) Orson Scott Card is a writer like that. Every book says "Onward for the good of humanity. Explore, multiply, and create!" He largely writes with a single purpose, at least it seems that way to me. If you are such a writer, more power to you. Card is a great writer and a favorite of mine since childhood. It is not a bad thing to emulate him in his singularity of purpose.

If you are like most writers, however, you will probably have a different underlying purpose for each major work that you undertake. You are not now the same person that you were five years ago, and that is probably a good thing. Life is growth and change, and your writing can and should reflect that. Even when we look back at the greats, the classics, and the ancients we can see development of purpose.

I think of John Donne, the magnificent English poet, and arguably the deftest handler of the English language who ever touched ink to paper. In his early years the purpose behind his work was self-serving, intending to show off his own cleverness or to poke fun at what he saw as the inconstancy of women. Later in his life his work became more romantic, more sentimental, and it sought to praise the opposite sex and the love that he had once found to be so trifling. Towards the end of his life Donne had become a deeply religious man, and the purpose behind his later works was to commune with his Creator, confessing his sins, praising God's holiness, and marveling at divine forgiveness and love.[2]

The constant throughout the change is that Donne's work was always full of purpose, and so it was always rich and full, even when it was flippant. Your purpose for your first novel will likely not even resemble your purpose for your last, but if you hope to have any kind of impact on your reader whatsoever, you need to know what it is, and write from that place of purpose.

Finally, by way of giving you one more piece of advice to help you find your purpose in whatever project you are now contemplating, I give to you the words of the marvelous songwriter Jon Foreman:

"...the moment I encounter something that feels difficult, I feel like that's when, for me, I turn to writing and thinking and maybe a song comes from that."[3]

Action Items:

In order to guide you as you consider and labor upon your book idea, I will be giving you action items at the end of each chapter in this first part of the book. The first assignment is simple. Find your purpose.

#1 Ask yourself, "Why am I writing this book?" It is perfectly alright if you don't know yet. Think about it for a couple of days, consult your friends. Ultimately, you are the one who decides. When you feel that you've found it, buy a notebook and move on to #2.

#2 Write down your purpose in streams of consciousness (just writing down whatever comes to mind) in your notebook. Don't be afraid to rant here. This is for your use only, and people will only see it if you decide to show it to them (probably don't). Get it all out, hold nothing back.

#3 Read over what you've written, and on another page condense it into a single sentence under the heading "Purpose." Don't write anything else on this page. If someone asks you why you are writing this book, be able to answer with a single sentence. Not two, not five. One. This reduction will focus you and help you get started in the right direction.

Chapter Two: Dr. Know

preparing to create

Another chapter, another bad pun to start it off. I'd like to say that I can't be held responsible for this one, but, well, it just isn't true. Yet like before, there is a reason for it, and I wager that it will help you remember the content of this chapter.

I have a little scenario for you to start things off. Imagine what this might look like:

Your city by the ocean has recently built a nuclear power plant. Two gigantic smoke stacks rise up from the ground and a technical wonderland of complicated machinery surrounds them. You are underground, descending in an elevator, and the elevator stops. The bell dings and the doors open. Security takes a look at your pass and you're shown into your office. It's your first day as an engineer working on the fission reactor.

Your new boss, a hearty Scotsman with a full beard and a neatly pressed white button up, greets you enthusiastically and shows you to your seat. A great wall of glass is spread out before you, allowing you to see all of the goings on inside while you work. Your boss informs you that someone will be along to train you straight away.

There is a lot of anticipation now. You've always wanted to work in such an innovative, scientific setting. You're excited and ready to go.

That is, until the man who is to train you shows up. He has a few days of stubble on him, coffee stains galore on his wife-beater tank top, and his forearm bears a tattoo of the word "BEER." You are surprised, but you figure that the man must be quite a genius to get away with such an unkempt appearance. You give him the benefit of the doubt.

Then, as he begins your training, something seems terribly wrong. He's speaking in vague generalities. You know more than he does. After some prodding, he finally admits that he's never worked in nuclear physics before. He was sleeping in the gutter and he decided that he wanted a job, so he wandered in and now he's training you.

Some of you are thinking, "Ridiculous!" Others are thinking, "Sounds like my job."

It is completely absurd, of course. No one would ever allow a hobo to wander in off of the street and lecture people on nuclear safety. No one would allow a very educated person to do the same thing if they were ignorant in the particular realm of knowledge that was relevant to the task. It's really a stupid hyperbole, isn't it?

So let me ask you this: how much research have you done for your novel?

Be the Expert

Yes, you may be very intelligent and you can answer the daily doubles on *Jeopardy* and your junior year English teacher once said that you have "a lot of potential." But none of that means that you have gathered the tools necessary for success for the *particular* creative work you are now undertaking. Are you writing a Western? Have you studied the Old West? I mean actually studied it?

If the answer is no, maybe back up a few steps and take things back to the beginning.

Why am I hammering this point? Is it so

important? Maybe you're saying, "Sure, I get that if you're writing some sort of specific nonfiction, like, say- how potato farmers ought to be treating their soil in the southeastern quadrant of Idaho. But I'm writing fiction! I don't need to go and hit the books."

Wrong. You do need to go and hit the books. Great writers research. If you haven't read at least three books pertaining to the setting or plot or *something* having to do with your creative work I would be skeptical that you are ready to begin. Otherwise your reader many turn out to be the control engineer and you find yourself as the hobo trying to pass off vague generalities as helpful knowledge. If you have spent years of your life actually *engaging* in a particular activity or with a realm of knowledge than that is even better, but if you're delving into new worlds, read a book. Read three books.

What we're dealing with is essentially this: don't be surface level. The surface is boring. Everyone can see it already. Dive in a little bit and take your readers on a journey. Show them Atlantis. They already know what the tide looks like.

Justification for the Pun

The greatest spy novelist of all-time is probably Ian Fleming, the famed author of the James Bond series. *Casino Royale, From Russia, with Love, You Only Live Twice, Goldfinger*, and yes, *Dr. No* are just a few among many titles that have earned him international acclaim and success. He is credited as being one of the best-selling fiction writers of all time.[4] Even today, nearly sixty years after his death, he continues to sell books and their film adaptations continue to smash the box office every time. There is such an excitement about his works. Why is that?

Partially it is the character he's created. James Bond is the original smooth-operating ladies man who saves the world by diffusing a bomb with one second left on the timer. People like that. But also it's the world that Fleming created. It's so full of mystery and double-crossings, international scandal and cover-up, assassinations and narrow escapes. It's enthralling. How did Fleming consistently create such masterpieces?

Well, for starters he spent World War Two serving Great Britain as a Naval Intelligence Officer. He oversaw two intelligence units and was a part of planning Operation Goldeneye. (Sound familiar?) In other words, HE WAS A SPY.[5]

The man who penned the cloak and dagger dramas of James Bond, an undercover operative and a Commander in the Royal Navy Reserve, lived, essentially, the life of a spy.

The man had done his research. He lived it.

Gaining Ideas

Spy novels are a lot of fun. Lots of people write them and maybe you're planning one out now. However, unless you have some kind of special forces military experience or a storied past of undercover operations, you may want to do some research so you know what the heck you're talking about.

There's nothing worse than a bland spy novel. So many inexperienced writers attempt them without having any idea what they're talking about. People actually go and write about the military without having any idea how the ranks work.

Hoping nobody notices is a bad plan. People will

notice, but that isn't even the biggest reason why you need to research your subject matter- and not just from other novels. Understand that I'm talking about reading nonfiction.

Reading about your subject matter will give you ideas. It puts more colors in your palette, more tools in your belt, and it will empower you to write what you otherwise would never have thought of. For those of you writing nonfiction out there, I probably don't need to lecture you on this. For those of you writing fiction, poetry, comic books, and whatever else, however, this is something that is sorely lacking for most burgeoning writers.

A Notable Example of Great Research

Have you ever seen *Jurassic Park*? Most of you probably have. Have you ever read the book? It's even better.

It's by a famous novelist you are no doubt familiar with: Michael Crichton. Michael Crichton was a prolific and talented author, cut short unfortunately by a too-early death. Nevertheless, he wrote dozens of terrific stories and he remains one of the kings of paperback.

Pick up one of his books sometime, any one of them, and flip to the back. He tends to include a bibliography. His bibliographies tend to be over a hundred items long. Some of these are newspaper articles, some are magazines or interviews, but a lot of them are books. Needless to say, the man did his research. Reading a Crichton book is really fun, in part because you can't help but learn something in the process. In *Sphere* his characters speak fluently about what they are doing as they descend to a pressurized chamber at the bottom of the ocean. In *Thirteenth Warrior* his writing style matches that of the ancient chronicler he emulates nearly perfectly. In *Airframe*, a thriller taking place in an airplane manufacturing plant, it's obvious that he knows what he's talking about, and the book is more interesting because of it.

Michael Crichton was a smart guy, but he never worked as a flight engineer. Yet he writes a brilliant novel that deals with the subject because he spoke with people who work on airplanes. He read books and articles on the subject until he was comfortable writing about it.

It was not an "educational" book and it certainly wasn't nonfiction, but he understood the world he was writing in.

Getting Philosophical

If you'll allow it (and even if you won't) I'm going to get philosophical for a moment, specifically speaking to all of you out there working on writing fiction of any kind.

The world is big. The world is really big. There are places you haven't been, people you haven't seen, and flesh-eating insects living inside your mattress waiting to devour you. (What the hell was that about? –Ed.) Hey, great! My editor is back.

Anyway, the world is much too complex and detailed for you to have thought of it. This is a given. We speak of world-building as an art and indeed, we will talk about it in greater depth in the second part of this book. We praise men like J.R.R. Tolkien for the entire world that he dreamed up and we marvel that he could hold such a thing in his mind. How did he come up with everything?

Well, the short answer is that he didn't. I'm not accusing him of plagiarism, I'm accusing him of having lived on earth for what can only be assumed to be the majority of his life. If he plagiarized from anyone, he plagiarized from God, since He was the one who came up with the whole 'existence' idea anyway. Tolkien didn't invent language, trees, people, or the concept of war and honor and sacrifice. He thought up a lot of neat history and races and words, but his Middle-Earth is in fact, the earth, with some tweaks. One of the secrets to writing great fiction is to understand that every creative act you ever undergo is actually an act of what Tolkien calls "sub-creation."[6] You are rearranging things, drawing from the real world and then tweaking it slightly. The best fiction is an accurate depiction of the real world *plus* whatever creative elements you choose to incorporate.

Thus, at least 90% of your novel probably will be rooted in fact by mere necessity. Shouldn't you be in a place where you can write about real things realistically? Research helps us here.

Fantasy writers have a bit more freedom than, say, people who write literary fiction because a greater degree of "made up" is expected in the genre. Yet still, even in fantasy, research is of the utmost importance. 90% of the book is still reality, so you'd better write about it believably.

Personally...

I want to be as helpful to you in this book as I can, and so I will continue to share brief examples from my own experience as a writer.

I don't read a hundred books on the subject for

every novel that I write, but I always read several. For the *Starfall* trilogy I read a book on astronomy, I studied Latin, and I read every piece of military history I could get my hands on because I wanted to be able to write battle scenes in a compelling and realistic manner. In particular, I studied the campaigns of Napoleon and Hannibal to a great extent. Much of the large-scale tactics and outcomes of the large battles in my trilogy came from Waterloo and Cannae. It was immensely helpful.

For *The Weathermen* I plopped a meteorology textbook on my lap and read it from cover to cover. I had some vague ideas about how the weather worked before, but after I read that dang textbook you better believe that I was in a better place to write. It gave me ideas for how the Weathermen's abilities would actually work, what sort of situations my characters might find themselves in, and perhaps most importantly, it gave me confidence in my competence to write it.

For Whom the Sun Sings was a slightly different process for me. I didn't read as many books as normal, but I listened to blind people talk about their experience. I looked at pictures of a blind person's eyes. I learned how to walk with a cane and how to count my steps. I asked questions, I found answers, and I immersed myself in the subject to better understand what I was going to be writing about. Without the research I did, I would never have been able to create the world that resulted.

Incidentally, if you are ever curious what it is like to be a blind person, there's this guy on YouTube named Tommy who has been blind since birth. He's a charming, self-effacing guy who will make you laugh as he laughs himself. He has a channel called the Tommy Edison Xperience where he answers people's questions that they are too afraid to ask about the blind. Sometimes they're deep questions, like "how do you experience dreams?" Sometimes it's not so deep, like "can blind people draw?" (The short answer is no.) It's worth checking out if you're interested. The way I treated color in my book is in large part due to hearing Tommy Edison's thoughts on the matter.

Before You Protest...

I know what some of you are thinking. "I don't want to go and read a bunch of books about gunfighters, I just want to write a crazy story about it!" I have something to say to you.

First, stop using the word "crazy" like that. It makes you sound silly. Second, if your subject matter doesn't interest you enough to read about it for a couple of weeks, then please, do us all a favor and don't write about it. Maybe you're not interested in a publishing deal, awards, and throngs of fans (frankly, those are bad reasons to want to write anyway), but believe me, even if you're just doing this as a hobby your writing is going to be a richer experience if you do it on purpose. Having fun with the research is a great way to have fun with the writing.

Choose a setting and a topic that is so interesting that you're *dying* to research it, that you're yearning to learn more about. It will make your book better and it will make writing more enjoyable.

What I want for you is to have more than you need when you begin writing. That way you can pick the best parts and put your action around it. Be interesting, be the expert, research before you write.

One last word of wisdom, partially because it applies and partially because I'm hoping people start quoting me. (You're being too honest! Stop it! −Ed.) I've long said that if you want to write songs, read poetry, and if you want to write fiction, read history. This comes from an understanding that creativity is actually sub-creation. You'll have a better understanding of the derivative if you have a better understanding of the original equation, of your fiction's integral.

Or, for those of you who don't like the math analogy, I'll say it this way: Know a father and you'll gain understanding of his son.

Action Items:

#1   Pick two or three aspects of the world surrounding your story. It could be a setting, a character's profession, a historical event, or anything.

#2   Find a couple of books on the subject and read them. Take notes in your notebook that you got back in chapter one. Whatever seems relevant to you, jot it down. Have a section labeled "Ideas" so that when your research gives you flash of insight you can save it in your notebook right then and there.

#3   Talk to people who understand the subject matter better than you do. Interview them. Ask their opinion. Ask them about particular aspects of your plot or a character's personality, or a character's job. See if they think it's realistic, fanciful, fun, or ignorant. Talk to more than one person. You'll learn all sorts of things and be better prepared for your writing.

Chapter Three: Follow That Character!
populating your literary world

There are two very important lessons in life and in writing. People will tell you the first, but they usually forget the second. Some stress the second and forget the first. Very few people will ever tell you both.

1. *Don't judge a book by its cover*
2. *Understand that other people are going to judge a book by its cover*

When I was first starting out as a writer, I was very poor (Imagine that). I dedicated myself to a full time schedule of writing and studying, and as a result, I didn't have two nickels to rub together. I always used to think that was a strange expression. Why would someone want to rub two nickels together? Well, now I know why. For warmth.

Just kidding. But really, I didn't have any money. I had some pretty decent clothes that had been given to me, however: hand-me-downs from an uncle with impeccable and constantly changing designer tastes. And he happens to be exactly the same size as me. (Thanks Uncle Paul!) All that to say, I literally had less than a dollar to my name, but I used to dress well, in part, as a defiance to my circumstances. I figured that I should always put my best foot forward no matter what was going on, and so that is what I did.

I was living in Los Angeles at the time and I carpooled down to San Diego with my big brother and my sister-in-law so we could visit my family. My brother is an extremely intelligent man, and he's done pretty well for himself ever since he left college (without a cent of debt). He's a computer programmer, an entrepreneur, and occasionally a real estate investor.

My sister-in-law suggested that we stop for lunch and my brother agreed. I, however, was in the backseat hoping to God that they would either offer to pay or that I could come up with some sort of believable lie as to why I wasn't eating. That was the worst.

Anyway, we park the car down in Seaport Village and walk into a seaside restaurant. I'm wearing Uncle Paul's clothes: Boss pants, leather belt, Express button down, and Italian shoes with a little shock of gel in my hair to give it that superman curl. My much more successful older brother was wearing cargo shorts, white cross-trainers, and a t-shirt that didn't really fit.

Something incredible happened when we arrived.

The host looked me in the eyes whenever he spoke. He asked me where we wanted to sit, he handed me the menu first, he served me my meal first, and when it was time to go, he handed me the check.

Me! Me, who's sitting there praying, "God, I really don't want to have the whole, 'gee, looks like I'm fresh out of money' conversation. Please let them pick up the check. *PLEASE* let them pick up the check." And then who does the waiter assume is the big spender at the table? Yours truly. I didn't even see it when he handed me the check because I was too busy looking at the ground for a couple of nickels to rub together. (Kidding.)

The whole time this waiter is ignoring my brother and my sister-in-law and paying attention to me, and they're the ones with the money! They're the ones who are deciding how big of a tip he gets, not me. He judged us based on our clothes, and his assumptions were exactly the opposite of reality. I knew two things then: that I shouldn't base my opinions of others off of their appearances, and that other people do it whether I like it or not, so I better present myself in a certain fashion if it is going to help me.

Incidentally, my brother graciously picked up the check without ever even glancing my way. He knew I was struggling back then and he didn't see the need to make me feel uncomfortable. What a class act. Be like my brother, readers.

Relating to Writing

Let's talk about characters.

1. *Just like they do in real life, your readers will judge your characters based off of superficial, initial impressions*
2. *If your writing is good, there will end up being more to that character, just like in real life.*

Back to real life for a second:

A friend of mine used to work a retail job with a guy I'll call Martin. She thought he was lazy, never picking up the slack, counting down the minutes to the end of his shift every day. Martin, in her mind, was not a real motivated guy and more than a little bit selfish.

Fast-forward a couple months and Martin is killing it. He's hustling, taking responsibility, getting other workers to work harder, and his attitude is awesome. Martin lands himself a promotion. My friend, shocked at the drastic change, talks to him one day and finds out that Martin is the only member of his family willing to work. The rest of them stay at home on welfare, despite being able-bodied. They would be out on the street if not for Martin's job. He pays all the bills, he gets no thanks, and his family is actually hostile to him- actively ungrateful.

The poisonous home environment had gotten him down for a while, but he told my friend that he wasn't going to let other people rob him of his happiness anymore, so he was back to living life on purpose and enjoying the moment. He was still in the same environment, still providing for his selfish family because he didn't want them to lose their home and end up on the street.

My friend originally thought Martin was a jerk. Turns out he was a saint. He was just having a difficult time for a while and he'd been dealt one heck of a tough hand.

You never know with people. You think they're one way based on their appearance, but then they go and surprise you. When you find out why it all makes sense.

Your characters should be the same way, and you as the author need to understand them so completely that you can always predict how they are going to act and when they're going to change. They should be surprising to the reader and make perfect sense to you.

There's No Such Thing as a Flat Character

I hate to start off a new section by contradicting myself, but let me rephrase. There's no such thing as a flat character in real life or in *good* storytelling. There's plenty of them in bad storytelling. Heck, in crummy books even the protagonist is a flat character.

Let's define our terms: A flat character is one that

is only defined by one characteristic. The mailman is angry, the boy from school is smart, the nun listens to gangster rap. (Wes, seriously... a gangster rap nun? We're going to be getting letters for that one. – Ed.) I'm kidding on that last one. That sounds like anything but a flat character, and now that we're talking about it, I may end up putting her in a screenplay one of these days.

In any case, flat characters are simple, easy to explain. They have one dimension (flat) and that's it.

This stands in opposition to round characters, who are multi-faceted. They have many dimensions and cannot be summed up by a single characteristic. They're complex, just like a real person.

Traditional wisdom tells us that main characters should be round and secondary or incidental characters are allowed to be flat. I say that if you ever allow yourself to write a flat character you've compromised yourself as a writer and it will get easier and easier to flatten all of your characters, including those that are supposed to be more interesting.

I don't mean that the mailman who has one line of dialog in your three hundred page novel needs to have an epic monolog, but you as the writer need to understand him and his motivations. This practice will help you push farther with your main characters. I can't tell you how many one-dimensional *protagonists* I read about in the first drafts of projects that come across my desk. There should be no flat characters in your book, because there aren't any flat characters in life.

A Matter of Process

I'm talking to you about characters now not because

it's obligatory to talk about characters in a book on writing (strangely enough, there seems to be very little pedagogy dedicated to the idea); in fact, obligation is the last thing on my mind. We're discussing characters because it is the next stage in the writing process. You have your purpose, you've done your research, now we're going to build some characters.

Characters are People Too!

The characters in my books are real people.

Sounds crazy, I know. They aren't like you and me in that we can't just go and knock on their doors and have a conversation (unless I write some such scene), but their reality is not compromised in the least. If you want to write something great, you have to realize that your characters are real too. There are too many books (and films, and tv shows, etc.) where the characters are fake. Their motivations don't really make sense. They shift personality from time to time without a character-driven reason. They aren't real, so I don't identify with them, so I don't like the story. Your characters need to be real people.

What do I mean by calling fictional characters 'real people'? I mean that they have thoughts and emotions and a past. They have likes and dislikes and dreams and fears and hopes. Don't they? They should. They ought to have a personality and a predictable pattern of behavior. Oh, they should surprise your audience sometimes, but the audience doesn't have all of the information. You as the author should have it, then reveal what is relevant at the opportune moment.

You need to understand that your characters are real people. Build them that way and treat them that way. It keeps writing fun.

Past But Not Gone

There's a mass-market paperback writer by the name of Harlan Coban who happens to be a favorite of my brother, Trevor. Since my brother loves his writing so much, he often gives me one of Coban's books or lends me another. I'm glad he has, because they're usually a lot of fun, and the most recent of his books that I read, *Six Years*, can teach us a profound truth about our characters:

Your characters have a past.

I mentioned this fact in passing in the last section, but it bears its own discussion. Whatever it is that your character is during the time of your book's writing is not what he or she always was.

Let's talk about *Six Years*.

The book is a mystery about a man named Jake Fisher, who tries to pick up the pieces with an old flame only to discover that she is missing, several people are dead, and nothing makes sense.

It's pretty intriguing.

The plot isn't so much what we're here concerned with, however; it's the fact that the main character Jake is a college professor but he thinks of himself as a bouncer.

Yes, a bouncer. Jake is an academic at a prestigious school, but while he was still a student he had to work his way through college by way of a job. That job was bouncing at bars. It was a defining experience for him, even though it was not of central importance to the plot.

When he meets people, he sizes them up as a bouncer, not a professor. This gives him another dimension. This makes him interesting.

Your characters have jobs, probably, and there is likely a certain defining circumstance in their life that shapes the way we think of them, but always remember that your characters had a past, and that past might continue to affect them to a great degree.

After all, isn't that how people you know operate?

Some Notable Examples of Solid Characters

In Shakespeare's timeless tragedy Othello, we meet one of the most memorable and black-hearted villains in all of fiction. His name is Iago, and he loves evil for its own sake. He is so twisted that wherever he sees happiness he wants to ruin it, wherever he sees progress, he wants to set it aflame and watch it burn. At one point in the play he even states, "I see a window and I want to paint it black. No colors any more I want them to turn black."

On second thought, that may have been Mick Jagger. (It was. –Ed.)

Iago from Shakespeare's Othello is an evil, depraved, kill you in your sleep if he can get away with it kind of a guy. He would never just up and dedicate his life to feeding the poor and nuzzling stray kittens. Why? Because it runs contrary to his character and without a compelling reason for his personality to change, the reader won't accept it. Such a change would be cataclysmic in scope, so without a cataclysmic catalyst, the cat-loving philanthropist would not exist.

Shakespeare, masterful writer that he was, understood constancy of character and impetus of change, so his characters are believable. They are real people.

Let's look at another character. Think of Sherlock Holmes, the intrepid and ingenious sleuth created by Sir Arthur Conan Doyle. Solving even the most baffling of criminal mysteries from his flat at 221B Baker Street, Sherlock is poised, introverted, thoughtful, brilliant, and subtle. We know who he is from reading about his adventures. Imagine this: would Sherlock ever show up to a crime scene where a drooling, maniacally laughing fiend with a criminal record stands over a recently murdered corpse holding a knife in bloody hands and say, "I wonder who could have done such a thing?" He's never going to suddenly be an idiot. He's never going to be a babbling airhead who likes to hear himself talk.

He's Sherlock. He's smart. He's subtle. We know him.

That's part of the reason we love him, incidentally. We know him. He's real.

Understand Your Characters

There is a great degree of consistency in great characters because there is a great degree of consistency in people. That is, unless inconsistency happens to be their defining characteristic, as in the case of a schizophrenic.

People often want to push back against this concept for some reason. "My characters aren't *real*. They're fiction. That's the point." Well, if I take a lump of clay and form it into a pot, it's still a pot even though I made it.

When you're building your characters, you have to understand that you are making real people. It is an act of sub-creation within the pages of your notebook. Think of it like you're finding out who they already are as you brainstorm. Look for the truth as you create. Your thought process might look something like this:

"Let's see... I'm writing a book about Tom. Tom is a mischievous teenager who- No. No, that's not right. Tom isn't mischievous. He gets into trouble sometimes, but it's only because he never really had a role model since his father walked out on him. No, his father didn't walk out, he took a dangerous job, and Tom didn't understand why he would take such a risk, and even though his father was just trying to provide for his family, Tom sees the fatal accident that followed as an act of abandonment. Tom is a sweet boy, but he has so much unforgiveness toward his father and toward God that he manipulates situations sometimes as an act of rebellion against these things that he doesn't understand and doesn't think are fair. Yes, that's the truth. That's who Tom is. Tom is pretending to be fine, but he's angry."

Do you see the power in looking at your characters this way? It will invigorate your creativity and free you to search for what feels right about these real people that you plan to write about. Know all about them, understand them, and then you can think about writing with them.

Stephen King is unarguably one of the most successful writers of all-time. He is one of the highest-selling, highest-paid, largest-reach authors with more film adaptations of his books than just about any other modern writer.[7] His books are page turners, keeping the reader engaged from each moment to the next, wanting just to know what's going to happen. Why is that?

It's because Stephen is the King of understanding his characters. He once said this about how he writes, "(I) put a group of characters... in some sort of predicament and then watch them try to work themselves free."[8] He creates enticing characters and then he simply follows them around, and the results are gripping.

People are interesting to people. If your characters are real people, they will be interesting. If they are interesting, they will do interesting things, and the plot is going to come a lot easier to you as you work.

"But wait!" you cry. You pull at your hair and scream, "That all sounds fine and good, but I'm not having any luck coming up with compelling characters! What do I do??"

Get a hold of yourself, man! *Slap*

Alright, now that you've calmed down a bit, we can move on and I will answer your question.

The Simplest Pattern of Development

If you don't know how to make up real characters, pick interesting people that you know from your own life, change their names, and put them in your book as characters. (Um, Wes... Not sure if you can tell people to do that. We might get sued. – Ed.) My editor sure is annoying sometimes. Go back to Hawaii! (Gladly. – Ed.)

I mean it. If you don't know how to come up with interesting characters, pick an interesting person and there's your character. I would advise not telling said person that you put them in your book as a character, and disguise it a bit, but all of the sudden you are equipped with a multi-dimensional, interesting character to lead the action. Is John from your job at the post office a hothead who's always trotting in one girlfriend after the next and nursing an addiction to adrenaline? Do you feel like you know him well enough to know how he would react in any given situation? Put him in your book and write about it.

Yes, this is a crutch technique, and for you more experienced writers out there it may not be necessary. Yet isn't this exactly what every writer is doing at some level when he comes up with characters? The only difference is that a subtle and skilled writer will create characters from *aggregates* of people that they know, they've read about, and that they've seen.

Say I have a character named Julio Wong-Smith. Julio's sense of humor is going to come from my oldest brother. His personality is going to come from a friend of a friend. His intelligence is going to come from some sort of root vegetable, like maybe a potato. (Why do you keep coming back to potatoes? –Ed.) The point is that in this act of sub-creation, I draw from the integral, from the real world. My characters will be lifelike and believable, and most importantly, they will be real.

If you are just starting out as a writer, pick a person and make him a character. Don't use it as an opportunity to gossip or fulfill some weird fantasy of revenge against your coworkers, and don't get mad at people in real life for things you made them do in fiction. Use this technique as a learning tool and a means of starting out. For those of you who are more experienced, draw from several sources for each character.

Personally...

Perhaps the most adored character from my *Starfall* series, as I've come to realize from countless conversations with readers, is the gigantic and wise Incus- a Nebula (one of the races in the series) of the highest quality. Incus is tall, strong, very smart, and determined. He has a dark and a secretive past, however. He is the sort of person who feels as though he must bear the weight of the world upon his massive shoulders, receiving blows in due course to make up for the mistakes he's made. (In fact, this is why I named him "Incus." It's the Latin word for anvil.) He is a woodsman, a warrior, a loner, and a true friend to those few who have occasion to earn his trust.

He was consciously designed to have pieces of my childhood best friend in him, a mountaineer named Preston. I like that I get to say that my best friend is a mountaineer. It makes me feel cool. (It makes you sound like a tool. – Ed.) That's about enough from the editing department.

There was a little bit of me in Incus too. I've studied grappling and martial arts, specifically wrestling and Brazilian Jiu Jitsu for many years. Incus, it just so happens, is an expert in close-combat martial arts too. His temperament has a bit of my old wrestling coach in him. His grim determination comes from my father. His berserker tendency comes from a kid I knew way back in elementary school. Other parts of him are plain made up, or perhaps I'm just not consciously aware of their source.

The biggest piece of Incus was from Preston. As kids, he was the tall kid looking out for me, inviting me into the mountains with him, teaching me about interesting things, and showing me a more adventurous side of life. While writing, if I was ever unsure how Incus would react, I would ask myself what Preston might do in such a circumstance.

Incus is not what I'll call a "lift" character. A lift character is what I recommended to the less experienced writers earlier- where you lift a real person and give him a new name, then set him in your story. Incus was an aggregate of many people, but the pattern still helped me immensely.

People love Incus. I've heard several of my friends claim credit for being the inspiration for Incus. So here, at last, I suppose I've disclosed the truth.

Don't be afraid to try the same thing in your writing.

You Are the Protagonist

It's unavoidable. Whenever you write a book, you are going to be the voice. Nine times out of ten, the main character is yourself, whether you intended for him to be or not. He might be you plus a few extras- you if you had x-ray vision, you if you were born in Russia during a peasant revolt, you if you had hung out with the wrong crowd, you if you grew up as the Prince of Egypt. In the last case, you would be a cartoon. And you would sing. But I digress.

It's not a bad thing to be the protagonist. In fact, it will usually help you as you write to put yourself into the story. Imagine yourself in the thick of the action, feel the whiz of the bullets past your face, the sweat on your brow, the garlic on your fingers. Don't feel like you need to shy away from being the main character for the sake of originality. Rather recognize the fact that you are the protagonist and present your best, worst, or most interesting self.

Most people out there in the world don't have a lot of confidence. They are usually bright, unique, interesting people with at least several good and redeeming qualities, but a lot of people don't realize it about themselves. Thus, we are left with the all-too-common "Whiney Mopey Man."

Whiney Mopey Man is the main character in countless stories. He is the one that you are supposed to be rooting for, but you just can't really see why you want him to succeed. He doesn't really have a lot of great qualities and he's angsty. He complains a lot too.

I read the first draft of a script recently, I won't tell you who it's by, but it was written by a successful member of the film industry. He was not a total rookie. His script was essentially a love story between childhood friends but, of course, the boy could never get around to removing himself from the friend zone and fulfilling his romantic destiny with said woman who was in a serious relationship with another man.

When I sent him my notes on the script, I told him that I liked the "other guy" better than the main guy. That's a problem for a love story. Turns out his other readers said the same thing.

The truth is that you are the protagonist, so stop being so down about yourself as you write! Pretending that you're perfect is cheesy, and pretending that you are just a so-so person with no outstanding qualities is boring! Both aren't true about you anyway. You are an exquisite, flawed, sincere, sinful, kind, compassionate, occasionally irritating, fun-loving, wounded, wonderful person. Write from that understanding and write with confidence.

You are the protagonist. Since we want to write from a place of understanding our characters to better write for them, spend some time understanding yourself.

And never, ever let your main character be Whiney Mopey Man. I hate that guy.

Action Items:

#1 Label the next section of your notebook "Characters." Have a page for each main character. Start dreaming them up and search for the truth of who this real person is.

#2 Come up with an 'unnecessary' amount of back story for each character, whether or not you end up putting it in the story is irrelevant. You need to understand the people you are writing about.

#3 Just for kicks, take a page and label it "Character Inspiration." Write down five or six really interesting people you know. Maybe even choose a person you don't know personally but you've read a lot about, such as Babe Ruth or Ghengis Jerry, the infamous potato-hustler of Northern Idaho.

#4 Write down a list of possible names for your characters. Choose them deliberately or just go with what sounds good. Consider having a theme to your names.

#5 Read the next chapter. You're almost ready to start the book!

Chapter Four: Ender's Ending
Where's this thing headed?

A wise man once said, "It doesn't matter if you know where you are, as long as you know where you're going." And by "a wise man" I mean my buddy Preston, mentioned in the previous chapter. He said it because we were in the middle of the Sierra Nevadas, deep in snow, and apparently, lost. Also he said it in an Irish accent, which to this day none of us can explain. I guess sometimes you've got to go spontaneously Irish in the middle of a serious conversation.

Anyway, as sketchy as we thought his statement was at the time (as he was the guide on our backpacking trip), it turned out to be true. He couldn't figure out what the mountains around us were, he didn't know what the big frozen lake below us was, he couldn't find us on the freaking map- but he did know where we were going. Despite having no idea as to our then-present location, he got us to our destination.

So, Preston, if you're reading this book, you were absolutely right. Also, I have around fifteen IOU's of yours that I'd like to cash in. I mean, as long as we're talking and stuff. (Get back to the book –Ed.)

Spoiler Alert

There is a wonderful, intriguing, future classic by Orson Scott Card called *Ender's Game*. I'm about to ruin the ending.

If you really would like to avoid the spoilers, skip

to the next section and pick up a copy of his book the next time you get a chance.

Ender's Game is a sci-fi novel set in a future where Earth has just barely survived two wars with an alien race called the Buggers (or the Formics, for you purists out there) that discovered our planet. Earth's only hope after narrowly driving the invaders away in the second war was to begin preparing for the inevitable final confrontation straight away. Earth united as a single entity and scoured the planet for the most intelligent, the most promising, and the most gifted children to train from the youngest age to be military geniuses. Man's only hope was to produce another Alexander the Great. Extinction was not an option.

Enter Andrew "Ender" Wiggin. He's a small kid, but hyper intelligent. He's an anomaly with a fierceness inside of him that the scouts like. He's selected for the Battle School program which is the first stage of preparation for promising young cadets.

Battle School is a whirlwind and a delightful adventure. The odds are unfairly stacked against Ender from the start, and the obstacles only get higher because the commanders think Ender might just be that genius they've been searching for. They want to push him to the extremes of his potential. Yet no matter the challenge, no matter how unjust the terms of engagement, Ender comes out on top in every simulation, every time.

He graduates to the next level, which is a station on a distant planet's moon where he and the friends he made in Battle School are put through a rigorous schedule of near-impossible simulations in which they must command earth's forces against the Buggers. It takes everyone to the brink of their own sanity, and the final level is so shockingly unfair that

Ender almost quits then and there.

But he doesn't.

Instead he tries something crazy, and it works. They've beaten the simulation, but Ender is burned out. He can't possibly go on to the next stage of training. He'll refuse to serve the men who've put him and his friends through such torturous rigors. He's ready to tell everyone off and go home.

But the military men watching the simulation act strangely. They're crying and clapping.

It turns out the simulations weren't simulations at all. Ender and his friends were commanding Earth's space army, launched from the planet nearly the moment after the second war ended so that the final engagement could be on the enemy's turf. Ender saved humanity, and he didn't even know it.

What an ending, huh? What an incredible twist. Reading it in summary, you might think it sounds obvious, but believe me, as you read the book Orson Scott Card strings you right along and you buy it. The revelation is a shock, and you can't help but smile.

The Best Laid Plans

I haven't met Orson Scott Card. I've heard him speak, yet though I've never shaken his hand and asked him about *Ender's Game*, I can guarantee you that he knew the ending before he ever so much as touched a key on his keyboard. How do you write that novel if you don't know the ending?

Well, unless you do it very badly or do an entire rewrite that takes you a year, you don't.

Ender's Game is far from the only example. I think of the Lady Vin's copper earring in Brandon Sanderson's *Mistborn*. I think of the tragically-timed suicides at the end of Shakespeare's *Romeo and Juliet*. I think of Winston's tearful declaration on the final page of Orwell's *1984*. I think of potatoes, lightly sautéed in olive oil, sprinkled with smoked paprika and sea salt. Granted, that last one's only because I'm hungry. (I give up. –Ed.)

A Stark Contrast

We've talked about *Ender's Game*, now let's talk about another sci-fi novel. I don't want to bash a working author any more than is necessary for our education and betterment, so for the sake of this chapter I will change the author's name and the name of his novel. Let's call the book *Darkness* by Damian Dodges.

Damian Dodges is a favorite author of my good friend and medical professional, Paul Morales. Paul loves to pick up a nice thick Dodges novel whenever he gets the chance and get lost in the technical and scientific wonder that Dodges creates. Personally, his writing is not my favorite, but to each his own. Undeniably he is a player in the sci-fi genre. Let's talk about *Darkness*.

Earth has been invaded by a much superior alien force. In fact, Earth fought a war of defense, but they were defeated and enslaved. Throughout most of the book, however, a band of characters seeks to organize a resistance and to strike back at their oppressors from the inside! The odds are stacked way against them, but they have to succeed. Plans are hatched, secret missions are put into motion... and none of it really works. So how is humanity going to succeed?? We're getting to the end of the book here, how can man strike back at the much superior alien oppressors and be free once again?

Well, the book is about 525 pages, and around page 500 we find out that one of the main characters, drum roll please, is actually.... DRACULA!

Dracula?

Yes, Dracula. Out of nowhere, one of the main characters reveals that all this time, he has been hiding the fact that he is the immortal, living dead, blood-sucking Dracula. Then Dracula flies off and kills all the aliens and the book is over.

No, I'm not joking, and yes, this is what happened.

Ender vs. Dracula

Now, I will readily admit that I am speculating here, but I just cannot imagine that Damian Dodges set out at the beginning of the book to write himself into a corner and then have Dracula miraculously show up out of the blue and save the day. The ending feels cheap and vapid because the book had been building towards SOMETHING ELSE. That something else didn't happen. The reader was promised a premise and he was betrayed.

Consider *Ender's Game* again. *Ender's Game* also had a HUGE twist right at the end, but it *fit*. It was *planned*. The whole time Card was writing his novel he knew where it was going. Even though the reader might not and probably did not see where Card was going, at the end it all makes sense and he closes the book with a smile on his face and a, "Wow." Readers of Dodges' book probably closed it with a, "What?"

Ender's Game has won both the Nebula Award and the Hugo Award (the two most prestigious honors a science fiction novel can receive), it has been on and off the New York Times Bestsellers list for decades, has sold millions and millions of copies, it has been adapted into a big-budget box office blockbuster (say that ten times fast). It constantly makes the list for best sci-fi novels of all time, best books for teens, best books of the century, and an entire litany of other awards, accolades, and accomplishments that would be tiresome to list here.[9]

Darkness was, you know, published.

KNOW YOUR ENDING. Have something to work towards.

Outlines and Notes, Notes, Notes

It is true that there isn't one single correct way to write a novel, but I will present you with what I think is best. Some writers are *extremely* structured in how they go about planning out the plot of their books. Others are more organic, finding out about the plot as they go. Personally, I am not one of the extremely structured writers who will plan out every jot and tiddle of the story before they begin writing pages. However, even though I tend more towards the organic side of writing, I still outline, and so should you.

Knowing the ending is the most important part of making an outline. It's the big X on your map. It's where you're headed and where you can continue to point your feet even if you aren't sure where you are. I have probably beaten this point to death by now, but it deserves it! Know your ending before you write.

I do not think, for me, that it is practical to put every single plot point on my outline. I like to experience some of the adventure and uncertainty along the way as I write. Yet my outlines do have more than just the ending. I like to plot out the milestones before I begin writing pages. I mark out the turning points in the story, the twists, the game-changers. If I have a solid purpose in writing, if I've done my research, if I know my characters, and I know the big things that have to happen, there's nothing I can't write exquisitely, and it should be the same for you too.

Personally...

There are several different ways of building an outline, and honestly, it doesn't matter which one you use as long as you pick something that works for you. Personally, when I'm planning out a book, my outlines look a cross between the "bubble diagram" method and the lesser known "serial killer's manifesto" method. (No joke, I'll have notes scattered between three notebooks, voice memos on my phone, sticky notes with plot points on my desk, in my drawers, scrawled on napkins... You get the point.) Not many people have accused me of having an organized system of notes.

And yet, time and time again my writing is complimented for its structure. Doesn't that seem odd? What accounts for the apparent paradox?

In my main notebook where I plan out whatever novel I happen to be working on, I have a master outline. I have a character's name circled at the top (when there are two different or intersecting plot lines, I have one bubble for the character that best represents each plot line) and I bubble on down towards my ending.

For me, an outline is a bit of a living, breathing document in that I make and remake my outline several times while I'm writing- but I would never start without one. Having an outline gives me structure, even if it changes a little bit. It lets me have a framework for writing with purpose, as we discussed back in chapter one. My notes are crazy, messy, and if you ever have the misfortune to try and sift through them and figure out what they mean (incidentally, sometimes I also write my notes in code or in different languages. I don't know why. Thank God that writers are allowed to be eccentric.) I have nothing but sympathy for you. But you could read my outline. That would make sense to you. Everything funnels back into some sort of structure, and then I can get to work in a coherent fashion.

Creativity is messy. Good books aren't. An outline will help you to bridge the gap.

But I Don't Know What to Put in My Outline!

I hear your suppressed anxiety. A blank page can be intimidating, and you're thinking, "So I'm just supposed to sit down and orchestrate an entire book? Impossible! I won't do it!"

Bad dog! It is possible, actually. *picks up spray bottle menacingly* Don't make me use this... (You really can't call people dogs... they'll get insulted. What are you doing? –Ed.)

Ahem. Anyway. Let me tell you a story.

Once Upon a Time in Florence

A long, long time ago, there was a commission in Florence dedicated to the beautification of its cathedral. A very expensive, extraordinarily large piece of marble was purchased and shipped to Florence, where first one artist was supposed to work on it, then another. Yet no one could do anything with it.

Some blamed the timing of the project, others politics, and there were concerns that the marble was actually not of the best quality so many artists declined to work on it. Thus, the beautiful monolith for a statue that never was sat in a courtyard for years, untouched, unformed, as nothing.

And yet this hunk of marble had cost a lot of money. It seemed like a terrible shame to let it erode like a piece of granite in the sun and the rain, and so a promising young sculptor was summoned to Florence to take a look at the piece and to see if he would agree to work on it.

According to legend, this young man came, met with the commission, and was taken to the stone. He studied it, saying nothing. Then, he went home.

He came the next morning at sunrise and sat on a bench in front of the block of marble and stared at it all day, taking no notes and saying nothing. When the sun went down he went home. The next day he was back again at sunrise, staring at the marble. Sunset came and he left.

He did this for nearly three months, according to legend. Finally, one of the servants working at the palace where the marble was housed couldn't take it any longer and he confronted the young artist. He railed at him and said, "Why do you come here every day and sit, doing nothing? What are you doing?"

The young artist turned from the statue for the first time that day, shook his head like it was the most obvious thing in the world, and said, "Sto lavorando." I'm working.

The young artist was a 26 year old named Michelangelo, and two years later that hunk of marble was the statue of David- arguably the most magnificent piece of art that man has ever created.[10]

Dream a Dream

The story is possibly apocryphal, although Michelangelo was known to have some very strange methods, so it is not outside of the realm of possibility that this exchange actually took place. It is reported that Michelangelo's vision was so exquisite that he would not work in circles around a piece of stone while he carved (like most sculptors); he would pick a side and chisel straight forward until it was done.[11]

The point is, if you can dream it you can do it, but if you allow yourself no time to dream, where is your vision? If you have no vision where is your art?

There is an old Japanese proverb that applies:

> *"Vision without action is a daydream. Action without vision is a nightmare."*[12]

Believe me, I've read plenty of nightmares. Think also of what Henry David Thoreau said:

> *"If you have built castles in the air, your work need not be lost; that is where they should be. Now put the foundations under them."*[13]

Earlier, we considered the question of how to start figuring out what to put in your outline. My answer is this: sit and think. Have a little notepad in your pocket and take a walk. If you find it helpful, take a nap and direct your dreaming, then write down the best parts of what you come up with. (Perhaps not everyone will be able to do this particular suggestion.) Sit on your back porch with a cup of vanilla rooibos tea and imagine. Watch your characters progress like a movie in your head. Consider how you might accomplish your purpose in the plot points of your book.

Dream, dream often, and dream big. Then write it down. That is how you build an outline.

Action Items:

#1   In your notebook, label a page "Outline" and leave several pages after it blank, saving them for future iterations of your outline.

#2   Take a walk, sit in the sun, lay on your couch, and dream. Focus your thinking and your imagination on the lives of your characters, your purpose, and the world in which your book will take place. Take notes on whatever insights you come up with.

#3   Write your main character's name in a bubble at the top of your outline page and start writing down the progression of the story.

#4   When you are done writing your outline and you feel satisfied with it and whatever revisions you have made, it's time to start writing page one of your book.

Chapter Five:
Writers Write and Writer's Block
getting things done and overcoming obstacles

I have a friend that I've known since I was six years old. Let's call him Peter. Peter would hang out at my house a lot when we were kids and even as a young adult. Once while I was in college, I was visiting home. Peter, a few other friends, and I were all sitting around the table, talking and laughing. When asked what he was up to, Peter would lately tell people that he was going to run a triathlon.

On this particular day, no one had really asked him about it, but when my mother came into the kitchen where we were and gave him a hug, he proudly announced to her, "I'm going to run a triathlon." And everyone pretty much agreed that this was a worthy goal and more power to you and so on. We were all a bit skeptical, however. Peter was on his third fudgsicle when he made his declaration.

Needless to say, Peter never did a triathlon.

He sure talked about it a lot though. Now I don't want to go ragging on my friend- he's a wonderful person and a hard worker with all sorts of great qualities. That's why I changed his name, since I don't want to embarrass him with this anecdote. Yet I can't help but notice the startling dichotomy between how much people talk about a thing that they are going to do and how much they actually do it. I may be biased in my estimation, but it seems to me that the people who get the most done are the ones who, at a certain point, quit blabbing and start doing.

How many "writers" have you met that haven't

ever actually written anything of any length or significance? I know one such "writer" who has been talking about this book that he's "going to write" for literally years. Years and years and sadly I don't believe him one bit. Maybe you are one such person. It's not the end of the world if you are. We all need to get back on track from time to time, and I hope that I can help you get there in the course of this book. If you truly want to accomplish your goal of writing something great, there is a path to doing just that. Simply talking about it isn't good enough.

Ground rules: don't tell people you are a writer until you've at least written a book, a play, or a screenplay and not for class. Tell people that you aspire to be a writer or are trying to become a writer or are interested in writing, but until you do the deed, harsh as it may sound, you aren't one. With a little hard work, however, you can become one.

Writers Write

Louis L'Amour, the great American author of Westerns, short stories, and even poetry, had some great things to say about writing. Perhaps the most memorable was the simple, almost tautological statement, "Writers write."

Writers write. If you don't write, you aren't a writer yet. It's that simple. Planning is good and necessary and crucial to your success, but at the end of the day, writers write.

Stephen King was working multiple jobs, living in a trailer park, trying to juggle kids and his marriage, and yet he still found time to write every night. He is a writer. He has to write. It's what we do.

John Grisham was working full time as a lawyer, an

extremely time-consuming profession. I heard him say from his own mouth that his desire to write got so strong that one day he decided that he would wake up two hours early so he could get to the office two hours early and get in two hours of writing every day before work. People at his law firm just thought he was a go-getter trying to get ahead at the practice, but then they wondered why he wasn't producing extra work. He was actually producing extra work, of course. He produced so much and of such quality that he eventually quit his job because the books were paying for his living expenses.[14] Now he is extraordinarily successful.

John Grisham's first novel was not his best. Neither was Stephen King's, nor H.G. Wells', nor Garth Stein's, nor J.K. Rowling's. By the time I finished my first novel I was an infinitely better writer than before I had begun it, and yet I had to write it to become that better writer. I set aside time, put in the hours, and the results were more than worth it.

You're going to need to find what works for you, but when it's all said and done, if you're going to be a writer you'll find a way.

I'm going to give you some tips, tricks, and advice for how to get the most out of your time and how to accomplish your goals and write something great, but the reason why I begin this way with this chapter is to simply encourage you to do the feat, then talk about it later. (Particularly if this is your first major undertaking.) Imagine a little Shia LaBouf standing in front of you every time you think about writing ("Just DO it!!!!"). If you haven't seen the video I'm referring to, you will probably think that I'm very strange. That's alright. I imagine you've reached that conclusion already anyway. (They have. —Ed.)

Read on, and I'll tell you my ideas on how to

produce consistently, prolifically, and at a high level.

Consistently Creative

It is often said that inspiration strikes whenever and wherever it will, that you can't just turn on the inspiration valve and turn it off when you're done. Art is mysterious, rapturous, and unpredictable.

I'll agree that art is mysterious, rapturous, and unpredictable, but as any artist worth his salt (and certainly any writer) will tell you, if you can't turn inspiration on and off, you aren't trying hard enough. I am a writer. That is my full-time, life-leading profession. Of course I can turn creativity on and off. That's my job. I turn it on in the morning when I sit down to write; I turn it off in the evening and on Sundays when I need to get some rest. The earlier and much repeated statement about inspiration being uncontrollable is an excuse for procrastination and poor writing. Listen to what world-renowned choreographer Twyla Tharp says in her book, *The Creative Habit*:

> *"Creativity is a habit, and the best creativity is the result of good work habits."*

I don't know how that statement hits you, but it should be tremendously encouraging! Destiny is in your hands. You don't have to sit around and wait for inspiration to strike. Inspiration is all around you if only you will prepare, then sit down and do battle with the blank page. In the end, that page isn't your enemy; it is an opportunity. It is a wild stallion that will serve you until the end of its life if you tame it.

All this to say, you will only produce consistently if

you consistently set aside time to write.

Too many amateur writers (and honestly, too many professional ones) live flying by the seat of their pants. "When will I ever get the time to get some writing done?" I don't know. Block out some time in your schedule and then you'll have some. When you sit down to begin writing your book, as you are now prepared to do, (having developed your purpose, done your research, understood your characters, and outlined your story) pick a regularly scheduled block of time to write. It's terribly necessary.

Things that you don't schedule will not happen on a consistent basis. Writing a book looks long and scary for the first time, and if you don't set aside regular hours to chip away at it, then it is long and scary! But if you make a plan and stick to it, you will come closer to your goal every day, and you'll even have an idea of when you will finish each draft.

This structure ends up being the most freeing thing in the world. You are no longer a slave to whatever happens to come up on any given day. Your writing time is sacred, set aside, untouchable. You can do anything with it.

Personally...

Mornings are for writing. Many people have said it, and for myself I couldn't agree more. Mornings are not the *only* time you can write, of course, and it depends on the schedule that you set up. A good friend of mine and fellow author Levi Stack (*The Silent Deal, The Magic Trick, etc.)* prefers to write at night, as do many others, and that's fine. I like to write in the morning, however, for a few reasons:

- My mind is fresh, I have no worries about the day yet, everything is clean and new.
- I've literally just finished dreaming, so my mind is still in a state where it wants to wander, imagine, and dream some more.
- Crises don't seem to come up in the morning. My cell phone doesn't start ringing until about eleven or twelve, and by then, I'm already done with my writing for the day.
- Whatever I set out to do first always gets done.

I typically get up at 6am, exercise, shower, read my Bible, maybe eat some breakfast, and by the time I'm done with the morning routine, it's still pretty early. I get to writing when that morning chill is still in the air and I feel energized, full of potential, and ready to conquer the world.

Granted, I am a morning person, but I wasn't always. I think there is some choice to be factored into the designation.

I'm a big quota writer also, and this helps me tremendously. Depending on the project, I'm looking to write ten to fifteen pages every time I sit down to write. You know how fast you can finish a book when you're writing ten to fifteen pages every day? I can write a book every couple of months.

You definitely build up to a more rigorous quota, and I wouldn't recommend starting with some high and arbitrary number of pages or words you want to accomplish each day, because if your quota isn't based on reality it will only discourage you. Nevertheless, start with a time quota; block out a certain amount of time to write.

Time is on My Side

I like to write for about four or five hours a day. More than that and it really starts to wear on me mentally. For whatever reason, being totally focused and immersed in another 'reality' for more than six hours a day is exhausting and confusing for your mind and body. Don't get me wrong, I've done it. Still, unless you are under a serious deadline, I wouldn't recommend it. Limits vary per person and per project, but I would suggest not trying to write for more than six hours a day.

By the same token, I would recommend not trying to write for less than a two hour block each time you sit down to write. There is a certain degree of momentum in writing. I (and many, many other writers) get far less done in my first half hour than I do in my second. It takes a little bit of time to focus your mind and coordinate your thoughts with your fingers. Once you are lost in your own story, true creativity can thrive and flow through you. It has to be warmed up, coaxed. If you can only afford to set aside an hour a day, that's alright, but try for two.

This is something that will improve the longer that you write. It may take you an hour to get into the swing of things for the first few months of writing seriously. Then it will take you fifty minutes. Then forty, then thirty-five, and on and on until you find your groove. One of the best things you can do to improve your writing time is to use it consistently, because a certain amount of learning and improving is simply inevitable.

The important thing is consistency. Just like with exercise, perseverance is more important than intensity. If you have an insane schedule but you *must write*, then be sure to get in your twenty minutes a day, or your Tuesdays and Thursdays every week when you don't have to work, or your week off, or whatever it is. As Samuel Johnson (a writer from a few hundred years ago) famously said:

> *"Great works are performed not by strength, but by perseverance."*[15]

Chip away at your book. It will get done if you are consistent and you don't lose heart. Do whatever you can to set aside a regularly scheduled time to write every day.

Where to Write

Louis L'Amour, the great Western novelist mentioned earlier in the chapter and a writer known for his ability to churn out story after story, once said:

> *"I could sit in the middle of Sunset Boulevard and write with my typewriter on my knees. Temperamental I am not."*[16]

When I was young, I could not write if there was music on. Eventually as I progressed through school, I could write to instrumental music, but if the music had words, I couldn't do it. Now, after having spent years as a professional writer, I can write just about anywhere and anytime. I can write while talking to you about an unrelated subject. Deep focus is a practice, and the plain truth is that when you first start out you probably won't be very good at it.

That is perfectly fine. Go somewhere where your concentration muscles won't be strained. Your ability to focus will improve over time if you stick with it. Louis L'Amour wasn't temperamental, but maybe you are, and that's fine. Until you learn that deep focus that will allow you to write anywhere at any time under any circumstances, make it easy on yourself and be in a comfortable spot.

I can write anywhere I need to now, but it is still my preference to have a change of scenery now and again. Some days I'll write at home in one room, then in another room. Some days I'll write at the park or on a bench on the street. Sometimes I'll go to the library or head into the office where I consult on films. I like to mix it up.

Some people like consistency in their writing environment so that *where* they are becomes part of the writing process, a sort of signal for their brain to let them know that it's time to write. This isn't really the way I work, but it is the way a large portion of the population prefers to work, and maybe it's the same for you. If writing in different places sounds stressful or unhelpful, pick your writing spot and stay there.

Some people like to be comfortable when they write, and I admit I love an easy chair as much as the next guy. (Who is the next guy? You hear so much about him. He seems to agree with everyone's position on everything...) Yet I know that I get more done when I'm sitting at a desk or a table. For some reason, sitting at a desk or a table says "work" to me, and I do. It's probably the same with you. Try writing your book at an honest-to-goodness desk at first. See how it goes. If you think another location or position might be more amenable to helping you write, try that out.

The point is just that you need to find out what works for you, and if you stick with it you will become more flexible in the long run. Focus is a skill, and yours will improve with practice.

The Common Thread

One of the greatest lessons I have ever learned as it pertains to writing and life is this: excellence will come only when you give up the appearance of work in favor of actually doing work.

Sometimes, after I've been writing for a while, I know that I need to sleep for ten minutes to let my mind organize all of the thoughts I have whizzing around inside before I can do my best work again.[17] That sure doesn't look like work, but I do it when it is helpful. Sometimes after I've written a chunk of my book I know that I need to spend a day on my back porch thinking and staring off into the distance, so I do. That sure doesn't look like work, but it is, and my writing is better for listening to what I know I have to do.

It is so easy to be afraid that people will think that you're being lazy, but I've discovered something. If I'm not lazy, people won't think that I am. Also, who really cares what people think if I'm doing my best work, getting projects done, and improving my skills?

If you need to write in a bathrobe, do it. If you need to play Enya and dim the lights, do it. If you need to munch on cheerios, do it. If you need to have a little buzz on...

Don't do that one. Seriously, writing while liquored up is an awful idea, as the experience of countless writers across history shows us. For some reason, writers seem to be about four hundred million times more prone to alcoholism than other people.[18] The tremendously talented screenwriter Aaron Sorkin got so deep into using cocaine as part of his writing routine that it almost ruined his life.[19] Don't do it. Your mind is sufficient without caffeine, alcohol, drugs, or any other mind-altering substance. Sure, drinking a little may loosen you up and get the juices flowing, but then it's a part of your routine, and the harder you work the more you have to drink, and it's a vicious, self-defeating cycle. I've seen too many people fall into it and end up wasting their incredible potential. Just my humble opinion.

Fear

There is a reason beyond routine that people drink while they write, incidentally. It's fear.

Fear is one of the biggest obstacles you will have to overcome as a writer. People are often afraid that their work will be mocked, scorned, that they'll be regarded as a no-talent hack. The truth of the matter is that until you make it, not many people will read what you write, and therefore it's impossible to really be hated for it. Allow me to ease your mind. People will only mock you, scorn you, and regard you as a no-talent hack if you are very famous. If you are well-known enough to merit mockery, then you are no doubt making lots of money and half of the people who make fun of you go home at night and read your books under the covers.

People are weird.

You do need courage to write, however, and certainly humility. You can't enjoy life as a writer if you're afraid of what people might think. Don't worry about what others will feel, and don't let fear cause you to compromise your story to account for what you think people want to hear. If what you write moves you, it will move someone else too.

Alcohol is a cheap trick around anxiety, but it's a short term solution. It will come back to bite you if you let it into your writing process. Don't misunderstand me; I don't have a problem with having a drink now and then, but never when I'm writing. Courage is the real solution to fear. Anything else merely treats the symptoms.

Something Joseph Chilton Pearce said comes to mind:

"In order to live the creative life, you must first lose the fear of being wrong."

Write what moves you. Listen to your gut. Don't be afraid of being unimpressive. Authenticity is itself impressive. Find courage and write.

I Haven't Made That Much Progress...

I've written seven books now: five novels, a collection of short stories, and this one you are reading presently. I have only ever written novels by hand (the short stories and this book were both typed). Pen and ink and paper for hundreds of pages every time. What on earth would possess me to do something like that?

It's simple. When you have a limited amount of space on a page and you're using a medium that doesn't erase, you can't edit.

You simply can't do it. I can jot down notes for revisions in future drafts, but until I finish the first draft and then transfer it to the computer, no kind of perfectionism can stop my progress. The temptation, for me, is too strong to try and get every word perfect the first time through, and trying to write like that is a recipe for... well, for nothing. It's a recipe for frustration maybe, but it certainly won't lead to anything of any length actually getting finished.

Don't worry about making it perfect on the first go around. We'll talk about editing and refining in the next chapter. If you change your mind about something, make a note in your notebook and leave it alone. Get the story down first and then you'll be in a better place to emend it anyway, having a better understanding of the big picture. Most stalling comes from an unwillingness to move ahead. (That would be all stalling. – Ed.)

I promise you, if you have the courage to put your pen on the page and start moving it (or putting your hands on the keyboard and typing) you are going to get something done. Once you have something done, you will have more confidence because you finished something. Editing is the next step, but we have to do things in the proper order.

Write first, edit later, and you will marvel at your progress.

It Was Going Well, But Now It's Boring...

I heard this from a budding writer the other day: "I was having such a good time with my play, but now I'm in a place where it's getting kind of boring to write and I'm just not as into it as I was when I started." Plenty of you will feel this way at some point during the course of writing your book. Some of you may feel this way now. You know you love to write and you used to be so excited about your project, but now it just seems kind of tedious...

I'll tell you the same thing I told her. If you are in a place where writing your book has gotten dull, there's only one thing to do:

Mess it up.

I mean sincerely, totally, paint-cans-thrown-at-the-wall messed up. Think of the worst possible thing that could happen to the main character and do it. Think of what would ruin everyone's plans and write it. A hurricane destroys the town the night before the wedding. The boy who's been training his beloved dog for the talent show finds him dead. The star quarterback breaks his ankle falling down the stairs on the night before the championship game- or someone beats him up so badly that he can't play.

What do you do now?

Suddenly it's interesting again, isn't it? Like it or not, conflict is the center of a good plot, and if you're getting bored with your own book it's probably because you don't have enough conflict. You know what the least interesting story in the world is?

> *Once upon a time there was a beautiful young lady. She was happy and the birds would swoop into her windows and sing and one day she eyed a beautiful Prince who fell immediately in love with her. They married at a perfect ceremony and the people rejoiced. They retreated to a remote mountain cottage for their honeymoon. And they lived happily ever after.*

The whole time you read my little paragraph here, aren't you leaning forward waiting for the "but..."? Only there was no but. People like buts. Just ask Sir Mix-A-Lot. (That was offensive. –Ed.)

Throw a twist into your story if it's boring, because let me assure you if writing it was boring, reading it is going to be like watching paint dry. Mess it up! Necessity really is the mother of invention, and if you suddenly give yourself problems to solve, the writing process– and the book– is going to get a lot more interesting.

If The Writers Block, Who Tackles?

I want to address the age-old questions, two of the most common inquiries I get as a writer: "Aren't you afraid of running out of ideas?" and "What do you do about writer's block?"

I think it's a pretty strange question to ask a person you've just met at a party. Why not bring up the worst fear of an individual the first moment you meet him? I think if we did this with other professions, it would look something like this:

> **Me:** So, John, what do you do for a living?
> **John:** Oh, me? I'm a chiropractor.
> **Me:** Chiropractor, huh? Aren't you afraid of accidentally twisting somebody the wrong way one day, giving them a crippling disability that eventually leads to gangrene and a degenerating spine that reduces them to vegetable state in the hospital? When the poor fool's children show up at your door begging for bread because 'daddy's not waking up again' what are you going to do? WHAT ARE YOU GOING TO DO, JOHN???
> **John:** Uh, I think I see somebody I know. Excuse me.

Just saying. Have some tact, people.

It is, however, a question that merits answering for writers. Here is my perspective on the matter.

I don't believe in writer's block. I deny its

existence. I don't want to sound arrogant, but I don't believe that it's a real thing. Writer's block is nothing more than anxiety masquerading as a thing unconquerable, or at the least it pretends to be a problem with the writer's abilities or the writer's process. Neither is true.

Writer's block has nothing to do with your talent as a writer, your book idea, or your writing process. It's a mental state of distress, almost always pertaining to something other than writing.

You could say that you have writer's block when you're having trouble putting ideas into words after your cat died, but I think you're just sad. It's going to be hard for you to do much of anything.

Writing takes a tremendous amount of focus, and all that writer's block represents is something robbing you of that focus.

My prescription? Set down your pen, close your laptop, and go deal with whatever is causing you the distress. When it's taken care of, you will be able to write again. As to the second question, you will only run out of ideas if you are too scared to branch out, research, and look at life with a poet's eye. In short, it is a ridiculous question and one that isn't worth your anxiety. Most fears are like that really. They're groundless when you take a deep breath and stare them down.

Don't be afraid of writer's block. It isn't a real thing.

One Final Bit of Advice

A good friend of mine, a man by the name of Reid, once asked me what writing a book was like. I told him that it was like reading one, only harder. It wasn't just a flippant answer; there's a lot of truth to it. Writing a novel should be an adventure. You should be excited to sit down and get into it every day. Will you be hesitant to sit down and do the work sometimes? Sure. But once you get into the rhythm every day it should excite you. Explore the world you're creating! When an intriguing question hits you, follow its path as you write. See what happens. Write like you read, and it will be a delightful experience.

When faced with a choice in your writing, make the interesting choice. Don't take the easy choice, the unnecessarily dark choice, the saccharine choice, or the 'I'm just a poor potato farmer from central Idaho' choice (??? –Ed.). Make the interesting choice. Think of some of your favorite books and stories. Aren't they surprising? They make sense, but they go in ways you didn't always expect, right? Do the same thing in your book. Take the interesting route. Have fun with it and don't be afraid of getting it wrong.

You can always edit it later, right?

Action Items:

#1   Find a place where you can be comfortable writing. Consider whether you are the sort of person who needs constant changes of scenery or if you like a more predictable environment. What do you need around you to write effectively? What makes it hard for you to focus? Create an environment conducive to creativity.

#2   Set aside a block of time in your schedule. Ideally, this will be the same hours of the day every day. Put this time in your calendar or planner. Write for the duration of that time five to six days a week.

#3   After two weeks or so of consistent writing, come up with a daily target of either words or pages that you would like to complete each day. If you miss quota one day, don't feel like you have to make it up the next day because it can stack up on you. Simply start fresh the next day, aiming for your quota once more.

Chapter Six: Touching Up the Corners
the editing process and refining your work

I admit it, I don't like editing. When I was in school I would always turn in first drafts and I was a good enough writer to get away with it. When a teacher would make us turn in multiple drafts instead of just giving us time to 'write another draft' I would stare at my pages annoyed, and then I would make enough word switches to reluctantly call it another draft. Maybe it's the same way with you. "My first draft was brilliant! If I had wanted to say something different I would have *said* it!" you say.

Calm down, Hemingway. Everyone edits. Even the greats, even organic writers, even me, even though it isn't my favorite part of the process. If you want your writing to be the best it can possibly be, so will you. You aren't done until you've done a good spell of editing: first by you, then by other people, then by a professional, then by you again.

It's true, writing the manuscript was indeed the vast majority of the work. Most of what you wrote will probably stick. You've painted all of the walls in the room except for those little spaces in the corner and between the crown molding.

Now it's time to touch up the corners. Dip your brush in the bucket and let's get all those little spaces we missed with the roller.

Your First Round of Editing

Let me be the first to congratulate you on finishing your manuscript! It's a great accomplishment, and it sets you apart from the 90% of people who call themselves "writers" despite never having come up with anything longer than a shopping list. Whenever I finish a first draft of a book, I celebrate, and you should too. It's an accomplishment, and I'm proud of you. Even if your book is about potatoes.

Now, the dust settles and you're ready to get back to your desk and take a look at this thing you've created (Hopefully two or three weeks after you've finished the first draft. You need some mental space between the writing and the editing to do the latter well). Where to begin? Maybe it's not ready to show to other people yet (probably), maybe it's already worthy of a Nobel Prize (probably not), in either case, it's still time to take a good hard look at your manuscript, and I'll give you the best editing advice you'll ever hear:

Pretend it isn't your book.

Seriously, please do yourself a favor and pretend that you're reading it for a friend. The writing process is very strange: while writing, you want to be as emotionally involved as possible. When your characters hurt it should hurt you, when your protagonist cries, you'd better be ready with a hanky for your own eyes. Breathe your own soul into your art while you're writing it.

When you're editing, you don't have a soul. You used it already, remember? You are taking a cold, hard look at this thing as objectively as possible. This doesn't mean finding fault where there isn't fault and it doesn't mean being overly critical, but it does mean that you voluntarily give up the right to look at your book like it's your baby. It is not your baby. You do not carry pictures of it in your wallet and bore strangers with stories of its first words. It's someone else's baby, and frankly, the kid is a little bit of a brat.

Orson Scott Card once said that there are two equal and opposite truths that you need to understand to have success as a writer.

1. Know that your writing is golden. No matter what people say, you need to know that your creative work is God's gift to the world, inspired by heaven, conducted through your hands. It is perfect, it is beautiful, and if anyone doesn't like something about it they are wrong and a fool and without artistic vision.
2. Know that your writing is garbage. It's trash that might one day be useful if some serious, *serious* refurbishing is done. Everything is wrong with it. There's nothing that doesn't need fixing. It's supposed to be a grown man but it's a baby pooing in its diaper. (Again with the baby metaphor? –Ed.) It's not good.

Paradoxical, I know. And people wonder why writers are so moody.

There is some truth in his somewhat hyperbolic statement, however. Yes, I'm paraphrasing him because I heard it from his own mouth while he was speaking and I wasn't taking notes, but if you give Mr. Card a call and ask him if my paraphrase was accurate of the words he said that day at the Los Angeles Festival of Books, I'm confident that he will say, "Who the hell are you? How did you get this number?"

Anyway, you need to guard your artistic decisions jealously while writing and hesitantly while editing.

I cheat a little bit when I edit since I write out my books longhand. I mentioned in an earlier chapter that this is so I cannot edit while I'm writing, but it's also so that I will *have* to edit when I'm finished. My story needs to get in the computer somehow, and typing up the manuscript forces me to revisit every single word. Most people's edits will be from reading, not hours and hours of typing and transcribing (Do my hands hurt while I'm doing this? Yes. A lot. Thanks for asking.), but the principle of the first edit is the same: You're doing a broad sweep over everything.

When you were writing the first draft you should have been taking notes. "Character B needs to have a mustache in the first chapter. Character A currently loves mustaches, but actually he should come to hate them by chapter four due to a harsh, mustache-related trauma. Character C needs to be better at cultivating his potato crop." Go through and read all of your editing notes first off. This will give you a place to start and will let you have some direction as you go through the writing. Keep a pad of your notes on the desk next to you as you sit down to begin a read-through.

- Fix awkward-sounding sentences. If you are unsure as to whether or not a sentence feels awkward, it does.
- Look out for reusing words twice in a sentence when you're reusing them. (That was on purpose, right? –Ed.)
- Don't be repetitively redundant.
- Cut the fluff. If it takes you nine paragraphs to discuss the love interest's dress, you're just wasting time. How can what you wrote be more concise while preserving the vision? Refine it. Also, if a dog in your book is too fluffy, make him less fluffy, unless his name is Fluffy, in which case it is okay for him to remain at his current level of "fluffy." (I hate you. –Ed.)
- Make sure that it is clear who is speaking during sections of dialog. This is almost

always a problem in first drafts. This will be easier to pick up on for other people since they don't know what it is you were intending on saying, but try and catch it wherever you can.

- Look for things that don't make sense. Brainstorm about how you can fix the problem. Rewriting and editing are an old married couple, and they get cranky if they're separated. They also get cranky if you mention old boyfriends, if the weather is bad, and if they're out of Metamucil. Don't be afraid to rewrite a section here and there as you edit.

This is your time to fix everything that you know needs fixing. If you are being honest with yourself, you know you kind of let it slide here and there, and that there's sort of a plot hole there, but it isn't really that important because maybe if-

NO! STOP IT! STOP IT RIGHT NOW!

This is editing. The time for coddling and rationalization is over. If it's broken, fix it. You might not know how to fix something right away. That's alright. Flag it and take a walk, or move on and come back to it. Just make sure that during this first edit (which might be one read-through, it might be five) that you fix everything you know needs fixing. Once you feel like it's ready to be shown to someone, it's time to find some friends who read a lot.

Your Second Round of Editing

First, some ground rules: This is not your opportunity to find people who love everything they read so you know that they will applaud whatever drivel you happen to scrawl across a page. This is also not your opportunity to reach out to an old friend who hasn't read a book since high school. Find five or six people whose opinions you trust, who have some sort of qualification as an advance reader (an English degree, someone who reads a ton of novels, a subject matter expert on a topic relevant to your book, etc.), and ask them if they would be willing to be advance readers of your book. Give them plenty of grace, but also give them a timeline. Tell them you would be honored if they would agree to read your manuscript and give their thoughts. Ideally you will print out manuscripts for them so that they have something to write on (or MS Word's 'Review' function is pretty good if they know how to use it) and you will be able to interview them once they are done reading. Encourage them to take notes as they go, be grateful for their help, and wait.

As brilliant orator Inigo Montoya once said, "I hate waiting."

Once your phone rings and you find out that your first advance reader has finished a read-through, rejoice! Then stop rejoicing and go have a sit-down with the poor shlup who had to read the garbage that you call a book, which is also sterling perfection and a work of utter genius and nothing is wrong with it.

Confusing? Good.

As soon as you have the chance, get your manuscript back from your trusted friend or colleague and go over their notes. Then, have a skype session, a coffee-date, or a lunch meeting with them. Prepare a list of questions and ask for their honest opinion. Do not appear devastated if they say something negative. Negative feedback can be extremely helpful. You asked them to be critical, so don't be surprised if they are, and certainly don't be discouraged. This is all part of the process.

Some questions to include might be:

- What was your favorite part?
- Which character did you like the best?
- What annoyed you about this book?
- Did anything not make sense?
- Did you ever roll your eyes while you read? When? Did you ever smile? When? Emotions?
- Were you ever surprised or did the plot feel predictable?

There are plenty of other questions to include, but that should get your juices flowing. This is also a great time to ask about those things that have been nagging you about your book, but you just aren't sure. Is Sally too ditzy or is she okay? Does Jimmy's decision to quit the team in chapter four feel believable or should you add a scene where his dad orders him to go and quit? Are you just feeling insecure about XYZ or do you have a legitimate concern that needs to be addressed? Now is your time to bounce these questions off of someone who isn't you.

A Quick Intermission

"Phew!" you're thinking. "The intermission is here, it's time to go to the bathroom and buy a piece of cheesecake."

I mean, I guess. Sure.

But my point in taking a quick break from the editing process is to tell you something that will help you tremendously when you are dealing with advance readers. Neil Gaiman, the British author and comic book writer, (*Neverwhere, Stardust, American Gods,* etc.) once put it perfectly. He said:

"Remember: when people tell you something's wrong or doesn't work for them, they are almost always right. When they tell you exactly what they think is wrong and how to fix it, they are almost always wrong."[20]

Remember this.

I got my degree in marketing back in college (Go Trojans! USC! Hooray!) and if there is one thing I learned in my market research classes it's this: people are good at knowing what they don't like and awful at predicting what they are going to like.[21] It is a strange truth, but truth nonetheless. When you do your interviews with your advance readers, you're going to get a lot of suggestions. Remember, you are the artist. If there's a problem, it's up to you to fix it. Every once in a blue moon you'll get a gem of a plot suggestion, but usually it's going to be an awful idea, so nod politely and say, "Yes, that is an intriguing option," and then never do it. Don't feel bad. You're writing the book, not them. You have the vision and you will have the answer. Don't feel like you have to take every single piece of advice that you hear.

To Neil Gaiman's spot-on quote, I would add my own rule of thumb: If one person says something is wrong and I don't agree with them, I respectfully ignore their advice. If two or more people are saying the same thing is wrong even though I feel like it's right, it's probably wrong and I should follow their advice and address whatever the problem happens to be. Everyone has slightly different tastes. Your crowning achievement in your book is going to bother somebody, but as long as they're the only one saying so and everyone else loves it, don't bend over to accommodate that single person's fancy.

This is your book.

Also, you're too protective over your story and you

aren't taking people's advice enough.

Confused? Good. We're ready to move on.

Your Third Round of Editing

After you have met with all of your advance readers, taken copious notes, and changed whatever needed to change, you are ready for your third round of editing. How should you go about it?

Hire a professional editor.

Don't pay through the nose, and be sure that you are hiring someone who's qualified, but do it. See what they say. It will take some time to find "your" editor, but you may as well start trying now. A professional editor is going to pick up on a lot of things that you and your friends will miss. See what they say. Why not? Review their advice, take the advice you think is good, and if there is advice that you think is bad, bounce it off of someone else. See what they think. You don't have to take every single piece of advice (unless you're in one of those contract situations, in which case, you sort of do...). Remember, this is your book, but just like like most people won't notice that the word "like" was typed twice earlier in this sentence, you won't notice a lot of the things that need fixing about your book. Other people will have thought, "Ha! I found a typo." Well guess who's laughing now, suckers? Hahaha! (Stop it. You're being petty. –Ed.)

Why will so many people miss the repeated word? Because your brain is really good at filling in the gaps. It's the same reason that there are going to be mistakes in the structure or the tone or in any of a dozen areas of your book that you won't catch on your own. You know what you meant, but the reader might not know. See what a professional editor has to say.

Your Final Round of Editing

Now that you've gathered all of this information, you've refined your work, you've gotten input from many different sets of eyes, you are ready for the big one. The final edit.

Your final edit will be similar to your first edit but more informed. This is a comprehensive, complete read-through which may actually be several read-throughs. Touch it up. Make it pretty. Make sure that this is something you would want to read if you weren't you. Be honest, be tough, take heart, and cut the fat where it needs cutting. Bulk it up where it needs bulking. Put a buffer and polisher on that sucker and watch it shine.

You've got yourself a book.

What's Next?

If you're looking for an explanation as to the best ways of getting noticed as an author, getting published, making a living, etc., you won't find it here. It's beyond the scope of this book, which is intended to deal with the *writing* portion since that is the part that is most often overlooked. Sure, there are a few tricks of the trade. You need to know not to mail your manuscript to publishers because it doesn't work that way anymore and you'll have to decide if you want to go the mainstream route or indie, but the most important step for success in having your work actually read is this:

Write a dang fine book.

It's the writing that is most important. Yes, figure out how to get it out there if that's your goal, but honestly, that subject has been covered well. Do a Google search and you'll be inundated with great articles on the subject. My aim in this book is to equip you as a writer, to give you a process that will guide you as you create. That is what is missing, I think. Creative writing isn't often taught well, and that is something that needs to change.

My Philosophy

I promised you a coherent, underlying philosophy in the introduction of this book. Some of the more astute readers will have already picked up on it, and even if you aren't sure at the moment what that is, subconsciously you may have picked up on it already. Nevertheless, it deserves plain speech and explanation. This is the underlying philosophy that will steer you toward better and more enjoyable writing:

Write from a place of abundance.

My grandfather was a brilliant man. He is perhaps the person who taught me the most about how to write at a high level. When I was eleven, he told me a story.

He was in law school and he had to write essays upon essays upon essays in class. They were almost always timed. He had to review arguments, build and outline cases, pontificate on judicial precedent and his own opinion, and he wrote furiously, as fast as he could. The only problem was that he was always running out of time. The writing questions were intense and difficult. There was so much to answer in an hour. His thoughts were regarded as very insightful, but he was having trouble finishing and getting it all together right.

After a test one day, his professor called him up to speak with him after class. He asked him about his studies and how the course was going. My grandpa talked with him and complained that he was always running out of time on the writing questions. The professor had noticed. That was why he wanted to talk. "Earl," he said (my grandfather's name was Earl), "I watch you take my tests and you always start writing too early." This was confusing. He just got finished saying he always ran out of time, did he not? Still, he listened. "If you have an hour to write an essay, spend at least the first half hour planning. It would be better if you spent forty minutes planning and twenty minutes writing. Then your writing will be better and you won't have any trouble finishing in time."

It sounded like strange advice, but my grandpa took it. His professor was right. When he started dedicating time to planning out his responses, the writing came easier. It was more insightful. It flowed. He was able to finish despite spending less time writing.

It should be the same with you.

Take the time to understand your purpose. Be able to say it in a sentence. Take the time to research your subject matter. It will give you ideas and allow you to have fluency in the world you create. Take the time to build your characters. Know them, understand them, dream about them, and put in the extra effort to make them real people. Take the time to craft an outline, even if it doesn't have every single plot point in the world on it.

Then, you write. Your writing will take less time and it will be better because you are prepared. Creativity is work. It's good work. It's fun work, but it is work, and it will be better and easier if you show up ready to rumble.

So many people seem to think that pre-writing is only hammering out every single possible plot point in the book.

Don't do that. It's stressful.

And yet prepare. Prepare the way I've taught you and you will be successful in writing your book to the best of your abilities.

Sure, there may be a clock and it may be ticking, but write from a place of abundance and you will get it done. Write from a place of abundance.

Write from a place of abundance.

Action Items:

#1   Do a complete read-through of your book and fix whatever you know needs to be fixed.

#2   Select a group of advance readers to give you feedback. Give them manuscripts, collect their notes, and interview them.

#3   Hire a professional editor to give it a read. See what he/she says.

#4   Do one more round of editing. Touch up all the corners.

#5   Start dreaming up the next book.

Part II:

Honing Your Craft

Chapter Seven: Adventure is Out There!
...and you're still in here?

Congratulations on finishing the first half of this book! Reading through a piece of non-fiction intended to help you become a better writer is a huge step forward, and I'm proud of you.

So you've finished a book- at least, you've read through the process of finishing a book, and now we must look to the future once again. We could look to the present first, but then we would have to go back to the future, and then I'm pretty sure Michael J. Fox would sue us. Or maybe Robert Zemeckis.

This second half of the book is about honing your skills as a writer. The most successful among us, regardless of profession, are those who never stop learning. They never feel as though they've "made it" in the sense that they never believe that there is no room to improve. Humility and a willingness to practice new things, ask questions, and grow are integral to your continuing success and improvement as a writer. Therefore, the second half of this book is designed to tackle specific aspects of your writing and life as a writer instead of taking you through the writing process. At the end of each chapter there will be exercises to help you practice. Let's get to it!

Well What Do You Know...

It has been said and repeated a million times that the best way to go about writing is to write what you know. I couldn't agree more. The problem, however, comes about if what you know isn't very interesting.

If you write what you know in that case, well, it's probably going to suck. (You can't say "suck." –Ed.)

Now, realize that this needs to be tempered with the understanding that most people sell themselves short in this department. "Oh, I don't have any interesting experience. I spent twelve years as a fire-breathing monkey trainer, but nobody wants to hear about that." Well, actually, I do want to hear about that. I don't know if you were spitting out sparks while training your regular old apes or if you trained fire-breathing monkeys, but in either case, do me a favor and write me some fiction. And call it *Simeon Volcano*.

Actually, don't. That sounds like a weird romance novel.

In all seriousness though, if you spent several years as a ballet dancer, that is a tremendous experience to feed into your writing. If you know what it's like to work for a terrible boss, that's not a bad place to start. If you grew up trading off spending months in Korea and months in the US, that's a pretty neat experience that most people don't have. Write about it.

You probably have some interesting knowledge even if you think that you don't, but here's the thing: we want to be versatile.

A Wealth of Experience

Sure, you might know all there is to know about how it feels to be the star athlete who leads the team to victory, but how are you going to write the shy loner who always struggled with coordination? You may know the backstreets of your town like the back of your hand (for example, three moles), but what if you come to a place in a novel where the characters need to hit the backcountry? Also, the "fish out of water" concept is really great in any story- are you able to write about that? Do you know what it feels like to be thrown into a situation, totally out of your element? You could make it up, sure, but is it going to have that same feel as if you were writing from experience? How do you become more versatile as a writer, able to write in many settings, with many plots, about many different kinds of people?

You can read, of course. We already talked about this in chapter two, so I won't belabor it here, other than to say this: Part of our job as writers is to read. A writer who doesn't read is like a conductor who doesn't like classical music, a dancer who doesn't like rhythm, a painter with no taste for color. A chef who doesn't eat. (That would be a dead chef. –Ed.) Read lots of books. It will give you a starting place and set your eyes on new topics to explore and new adventures to undertake. Read.

That said, we have already talked about research, or more properly, vicarious research. Yet there's nothing quite like living the adventure for yourself and writing about it. In *The Sun Also Rises,* Ernest Hemingway writes about the world-famous San Fermine festival in Pamplona and the Running of the Bulls. It all feels so realistic. How did he capture this unique, bizarre little town so perfectly?

Well, mostly it was because he had attended San Fermine and had run with the bulls himself. In Pamplona there are streets and pubs named after Hemingway, so famous was his visit.[22] He knew what it was like to sit in the arena and watch with a mixture of fear, morbid curiosity, and suppressed bloodlust as the matador takes the stage and fights a bull. He knew what it was like to have a two ton, angry animal charging down on him. He knew what it smelled like.

He knew the feeling of the air. He knew the palpitations of his own heart, felt the sweat dripping down his brow. All of these experiences were not just ideas to Hemingway. They were memories. He wrote about them beautifully in fiction.

Method Acting, Method Writing

I've tried to keep my examples mostly restricted to books, but every once in a while the perfect illustration comes from the film world. (Give me a break- I work in a film studio.) (No. -Ed.) When talking about living the adventure, one man leaps to my mind, surging to the forefront, begging to be mentioned. That man is Daniel Day Lewis.

Daniel Day Lewis might just be the most incredible actor alive today. People will always disagree about who the best is, of course, but you'll be hard-pressed to find someone who isn't extremely impressed by his work. He is the only male actor *in history* to receive the Oscar three times for Best Actor[23] (*My Left Foot, There Will Be Blood, Lincoln*) and one of only three male actors to receive three Oscars. He is perhaps best known for his portrayals of Bill the Butcher in *Gangs of New York*, Christy Brown in *My Left Foot*, Daniel Plainview in *There Will Be Blood*, Hawkeye in *Last of the Mohicans*, and Abraham Lincoln in *Lincoln*. He has received the highest awards and accolades[24] from everyone of importance- the Screen Actors Guild, the Golden Globes, the Academy, the British Academy, and he was even knighted.[25]

That's right. Daniel Day Lewis is such a great actor that he was knighted.

Great actors play to the camera very well and can produce tear-jerking performances time and time again. However, most great actors play the same role over and over again in a different setting. Think of somebody like William H. Macy. He's incredibly talented, but when you really look at the films he's been in, he basically plays one role: William H. Macy. I'm not picking on him in particular. I think of Denzel Washington, Tom Cruise- these are superb actors. It isn't necessarily a bad thing. Actors act.

But Daniel Day Lewis, he transforms.

Every film I have ever seen him in presents an entirely different person. Christy Brown does not have a single mannerism in common with Hawkeye. Bill the Butcher and Daniel Plainview, who could have been portrayed very similarly by a lesser actor, were completely different. In *Lincoln*, Lewis *was* our sixteenth President. It was incredible. There are very few actors who can do the sort of transformation that Daniel Day Lewis does. None do it so well. He is an anomaly.

He is also a method actor.

Method Acting: noun. A dramatic technique in which actors identify as closely as possible with the character played by correlating experiences from their personal lives to the character; also called Stanisklavsky system.[26]

Daniel Day Lewis takes it a step further than most method actors even. He actively seeks out experiences that will help him understand the part he is playing, the fiction he is creating through his acting. When preparing to play Hawkeye for *Last of the Mohicans*, he went out and built a canoe, learned how to shoot period-specific weapons, and learned how to trap and skin animals. He was now the kind of man who goes to the woods and builds canoes, shoots muskets, and skins animals. While on set for *My Left Foot*, in which he portrayed a writer with severe cerebral palsy, Daniel Day Lewis would not walk onto the set. He had to be carried. He lived as though he had cerebral palsy for months so that he would understand his character.[27]

That's commitment, and the results speak for themselves.

Why not be a method writer?

I'm not saying rent a wheelchair, unless that helps you in some way. I'm saying go and seek out experiences that will help you understand what you are writing about. Let's keep it legal and let's keep it ethical, but there is a world of opportunity and experience out there waiting to make a better writer out of you- and a more interesting person too.

"Do it!" – Emperor Palpatine*
*original quote by Shia Labouf

I want to encourage you to do something different. Looking for ideas for your next book? Go and do something you've never done before. Sign up for a gymnastics course. Learn what your body is capable of and watch others. If you're that excellent athlete who doesn't know what it feels like to be picked last, pick a sport your skills might not transfer to so well. Basketball star? Go play pickup soccer in the park. Or waterpolo. Or golf. Have a firsthand idea of what it feels like to be on the outside looking in, or triumphant, or frustrated, or elated. Know what it feels like from experience and it will make you a better, more versatile writer. Everything feeds into your creativity.

Let me tell you about one of my pet peeves when I'm reading: bad fight scenes.

I can't stand them. Writers often describe a fight in the most dull, impossible, and frankly stupid manner. I read a book once, I won't say the author's name, where a character's foot seemed to be bending the wrong way because the writer didn't understand his fighting terminology. A kick swung around backwards and hit the bad guy where? You see the same problem in a lot of TV shows. Bad fight scenes are the worst.

I'm particularly bothered by them because I've studied a bit myself. I've wrestled for many years and coached at the collegiate club level, peewee, and everything in between. I've studied Brazilian Jiu Jitsu for many years with some of the best instructors in the United States.[28] I don't pretend to be a master, but I have enough experience to know what I'm talking about. I know what will be exciting, what sounds good, and what's realistic. You don't necessarily need to spend years studying and training to write a good fight scene- but take a class or two. Spend a couple evenings a week at the dojo for a month before you write that novel where the protagonist is a kung fu master. A little bit of experience goes a long way.

I guarantee you you'll write better fight scenes after even one martial arts class than if you have never taken any at all.

Sure, there are some things you won't be able to experience for yourself before you write about them, and that's okay. There are always exceptions. Tom Clancy, for example, was never able to serve in the military so he wrote about it instead.[29] All I'm saying is seek out experiences that will help you. It will free you to write about a greater range of topics, which will give greater range to your characters, which will make you a better writer. Do it.

Jack of Trades, Master of... What?

I'm convinced that education has suffered greatly in the last hundred years or so. I read C.S. Lewis' *Surprised by Joy* in which he chronicles his early life and education. I've read a lot of his work, and one thing that Lewis keeps coming back to is that he calls himself a poor scholar.

The man spoke English, French, German, and Italian, not to mention the ancient languages he dabbled in, including Latin and Greek. You know what's astounding? For his day, his assessment of himself was not totally erroneous.

He was a brilliant man, of that there can and could be no doubt- then or now, but general education ensured that students in a good school system had a general knowledge of everything important and a mastery of a few things. Most people today have neither.

What I want to encourage you with in this section is this: be the master of something. Decide upon a skill and master it. Have you dabbled in the piano? Master it. Dabbled in break dancing? Master it. Watercolor? Master it. You don't have enough time to master everything, but pick one or two things to learn and understand completely. It will make you a better writer. The dullest writers in existence are those who do nothing but write. I have a bit of a personal distaste for a particular group of writers (now passed away) in the United States. I won't get into what group it was, but the main issue I take with many of them is that they wrote exclusively about life as a writer- to the point where they never seemed to get around to writing about ANYTHING ELSE. How boring. How incredibly dull.

A writer should be something else also. Master a skill. Let it color your lines. Write about skateboarders better than anybody else because you are one. Don't be one of those people who have craft but no heart, no soul, and no experience.

Kurt Vonnegut once told the *Paris Review*:

> *"I'm on the New York State Council for the Arts now, and every so often some other member talks about sending notices to college English departments about some literary opportunity, and I say, 'Send them to the chemistry departments, send them to the zoology departments, send them to the anthropology departments and the astronomy departments and the physics departments, and all the medical and law schools. That's where the writers are most likely to be. I think it can be tremendously refreshing if a creator of literature has something on his mind other than the history of literature so far."*[30]

I told you that we would be discussing ways of honing your writing skills in this section, and we will and we are, but this is important. You will be a better writer if you are involved in something, invested somewhere, defined.

Adventure is out there. Go and find some.

Bring a journal while you're at it.

Exercises:

For this second half of the book, get a writing journal to practice in. At the top, write what you're writing about/what the writing exercise was. Keep it to see your improvement and to gain insight.

#1   Go hiking. Journal about it later. What did you notice? What surprised you? How did you feel? What did you think about? Why do hikers love to hike so much?

#2   Volunteer for something. Soup kitchen, kids' ministry at church, reading to the blind, roadside beautification, whatever. Volunteer for something you would never usually do. Sit and think about what the experience taught you. Do it a few times, maybe. If it's something you find a passion for, do it more often.

#3   Sit down indoors and set a timer for five minutes. Write whatever comes to mind about water. Then, get up and find a pool, a lake, or the ocean and luxuriate in the sensation of swimming. Once you get out, immediately, before you're even all the way dry, set that same timer again and write for five minutes about water. Do you notice a difference? Compare your piece from memory and your piece from recent experience. For even better results, do this exercise built around an activity you have never experienced personally before.

#4   Next time you plan out a book, figure out a way to give yourself a relevant, method-acting kind of experience that will help you write it better.

Chapter Eight: Psycho
understanding how people work[31]

I was at the beach one time with a group of friends, and we got talking to this homeless guy playing the harmonica. He either played it really well or terribly. I forget which. Great beard though, I remember that much.

We were holding a fairly normal conversation with him until at one point he decides to tell us his secret. He leans in, looks to the left, looks to the right, and says, "I'm Jesus... sometimes." What? I asked him what on earth he was talking about and he said, "Sometimes, I can't control when- I'm Jesus." And then he went on to swear a lot and talk about things that made no sense and endorse Kanye West as President.

Clearly the man was crazy.

On the same day, a friend of mine was talking to someone else and receiving a lecture about how the world is apparently run by a group of omnipotent sea turtles living in the sky. "It's just that... they're up there and they control everything... And they make WAVES."

If you ever want to meet interesting people, go to the beach.

Man...

Those two people we met that day were definitely mentally ill. It's hard to track with people like that because we don't understand them very well, most of us. It's hard to predict what they're going to do, again, because we don't know what's going on in that head of theirs. It's pretty understandable when your average joe walking down the street doesn't understand how a crazy person thinks; it's even understandable that a writer might not understand how a crazy person thinks. Yet by and large, people don't even understand how *normal* people think. We spend so much time interacting with people, talking about people, trying to outguess people, when in reality, there aren't that many people who have made a decided effort to learn how their fellow man works upstairs.

If only there were a branch of science dedicated to studying the mind and soul, or the psyche! (Lame set-up. – Ed.)

There is one, of course. It's called Psychology. Yet despite the fact that we live in a world of such easily accessible information, I would venture to guess that only a small percentage have studied it in a meaningful way. Things slip through the cracks, understandably, but as writers a concerted effort to understand what makes people tick is a good idea. It will aid your writing considerably.

Why are we talking about Psychology in a book about writing? Because you will write better characters if you understand how people think. If you write better characters you will write better books. If you write better books, you will lose fifteen pounds and win Current Magazine's "Sexiest Man Alive" competition.

Well, you'll write better books anyway. (That was odd. – Ed.)

A Few Fries Short of a Happy Meal

A few disclaimers before we get into it: Firstly, understand that Psychology is what we can call a "soft science."[32] That means basically that a much lesser portion of it can be definitively proved according to the scientific method when compared to a subject like math or physics. This doesn't mean that Psychology is not a legitimate study, nor does it mean that it isn't worth your time, nor does it mean that *everything* is up for debate. Most of it, however, is up for debate. Studying Psychology requires critical thinking and sound judgment. There are a lot of different ideas out there, and some psychologists are probably crazier than their patients.

Secondly, understand that Psychology has an unnatural and unhelpful bias towards studying abnormal man.[33] Much of the time a Psychology class or textbook will focus heavily on pathology, things like schizophrenia, Alzheimer's, or Tourette's. These are no doubt interesting subjects and a great resource if you intend to have one of your characters be a few fries short of a happy meal, but by and large, it is more valuable to understand how the mind *should* work. When bank tellers are trained how to spot a counterfeit bill they don't study all the innumerable varieties of counterfeits out there, they study the real thing so well that they can tell right away when something is off.[34]

Finally, understand that Psychology has a heavy bias against the belief in God, whereas the majority of people on the planet operate under the assumption that belief in God is normal and good. According to a 2006 survey (Politics of the American Professoriate) published in the journal *Sociology of Religion* by researchers Neil Gross of the University of British Columbia and Solon Simmons of the George Mason University, Psychology Professors may be the least religious of any subject in the university. Solidly half of those surveyed identified as atheists and another eleven percent identified as agnostic. Very few were willing to say that they definitely believed in a god of any kind. Place that next to a 2012 Pew Research Center's Forum on Religion and Public Life study that states, "There are 5.8 billion religiously affiliated adults and children around the globe, representing 84% of the 2010 world population of 6.9 billion." We as writers should understand people's motivations. Psychology talks about the "phenomenon of religion" from time to time, but realize that the information comes from a field that is generally speaking rather hostile to the idea. Faith is a great motivator for much of the world's population, and regardless of anyone's opinion, we need to write from that understanding.

Now that We're Past the Disclaimers...

The worst writing tends to be that which has no understanding of the motivations of its characters. The best writing understands what is going on inside of its characters' minds and hearts and goes forward from that place. Reading up on Psychology can be a great way to improve your skill in creating characters and understanding them. This will help you write a compelling plot as well, since your plot is typically driven by your characters.

My intention for this chapter is to encourage you to be a student of humanity's motivation. What drives a man? How does a man act when he is desperate and has nothing left to lose? What is the most confusing aspect of the human condition? (That is a great place to start formulating a novel idea, FYI) Look at what people do and ask yourself, "Why?" Just don't do it out loud. People don't like that apparently.

Psychology is very imperfect, but it can be very helpful as a study on character. My intention for this chapter is to:

- Encourage you to ask questions
- Give you some resources and inspiration to study further
- Equip you to train yourself to write characters in a more compelling fashion
- Explain why Idaho's potato farmers aren't using enough compost in their fields

You thought I forgot about the potato joke, didn't you? (We *hoped* you had forgotten about it. – Ed.)

The point is this: you can't write a masterful psychological thriller if you don't understand how people think. I'm going to give you a brief overview of the different incarnations of Psychology mostly because I think it's interesting. There are schools of thought ad infinitum, ad nauseum, ad WHY CAN'T ANYONE AGREE??? Yet at its core, Psychology really divides up into four different perspectives. This is not a scholarly treatment of the subject in any way. Though many others will agree with me, I'm the one who sees it fit to split the various schools up into these four ideologies. It isn't canon, but it's a good back of hand heuristic.

Also, it is worth noting that regardless of which school of thought is most correct, your writing will be better if you at least understand one of them and write from that place of understanding. What is your theory on human behavior? What motivates a person?

What is fear, lust, hope, heartache, courage, creativity? Why do people do the things they do?

The Psychoanalytic Perspective

Dr. Sigmund Freud is one of the fathers of modern Psychology. You cannot study the subject without his name coming up. He was born in 1856 in the Czech Republic and studied to become a neurosurgeon. In essaying to better understand the brain, he developed a system of treatment for mental illnesses called "psychoanalysis" that serves as the basis for most therapy today. If you read Psychology from a psychoanalytic, or a Freudian, or a Jungian perspective (yes, there are some differences between Freudian thought and Jungian thought, but they are highly related and for our purposes, grouped) this is basically what you will be taught:

Man is in three parts- the id, the ego, and the superego. These are Latin words that Freud adopted to mean man's unconscious mind, his conscious mind, and his so-called "higher consciousness" respectively. The id is a raging, dark sea of chaos and animal instinct. The ego is who you are on a daily basis. The super ego goes beyond normal limitations of consciousness. In a sense, it is the ideal you. The ego is in sort of a struggle between listening to his baser instincts, the id, and his higher nature, the superego. Neurosis is caused by a discord between the unconscious mind and the conscious mind. "Psychic energy" comes up a lot, as does the concept of humanity's supposed "collective unconscious."

Symbolism, dreams, myths, and folklore play a heavy role in Psychoanalysis because its adherents believe that they are the way that man's consciousness communicates with its unconsciousness.

Man is a product of his environment. He acts in a manner consistent both with external forces as well as the animal instincts that well up in him from his id. Most everything is sexually motivated at an unconscious level, and Freud probably never said the line, "sometimes a cigar is just a cigar."[35] He likely thought that cigar was all sorts of things.

Treatment takes the form of understanding where a patient's thinking is incorrect and replacing it with a new way of thinking (namely, replacing it with Freud's way of thinking).

The Humanist Perspective

The big names in Humanist Psychology are Carl Rogers and Abraham Maslow. Humanist Psychology represents a break from Freud in a number of crucial senses, though it, like every other branch of modern Psychology, resembles it in others. Humanists have made it easy for us to explain them, as there are five basic principles of Humanist Psychology:

1. Humans as a whole are greater than the sum of their parts and cannot be reduced to their components.
2. Humans have their existence in a uniquely human context, as well as in a cosmic ecology.
3. Humans are aware and conscious, and that always includes self-consciousness.
4. Humans have the ability to make choices and thus have responsibility.
5. Humans do things intentionally, strive for goals, are aware that they cause future events, seek meaning, value, and creativity.

This list is a paraphrase, but you get the idea.

Humanist Psychology is heavily influenced by the ideas of existentialist thinkers, men like Nietzsche, Sartre, and others, as well as by Eastern philosophy. Man is at his core good. Therefore, if you can be who you are, you will be happy, fulfilled, and in a higher state of consciousness. The goal is to reach what humanists call "Self-actualization." Neurosis comes from ideas of self-incongruance between what an individual wishes they were and what they actually are. People have the freedom to make their own sense out of their life; freedom is at odds with any kind of limitations to the humanist.

According to Maslow, man has a number of different needs, but they organize themselves in order of importance. The base of man's needs are his physiological needs, without which he will not be able to seek out higher orders of needs. Physiological needs are things like food, water, sleep, and (depending on who you ask) sex. Once these are fulfilled, his next order of needs is for safety. This includes physical safety, but also security for his property, knowing his family is taken care of, employment security, security in his health, etc. Next comes the order of love and belonging, the need to be a wanted member of a group, a family, a friendship circle, and for sexual intimacy. The next order of needs is esteem, which is having accomplishments, the respect of others, and respect for others. The highest order of needs is called self-actualization, as previously mentioned. Self-actualization includes morality, creativity, problem-solving ability, spontaneity, and lack of prejudice.

This ordering of man's needs is called Maslow's Hierarchy of Needs. The operating assumption of this theory is that man's baser needs must be met before he can be fulfilled on a higher plane of consciousness. A man who doesn't know where he's going to sleep or if he's going to starve doesn't much care what people think of him, according to the theory. If someone doesn't feel safe, they're not looking for accomplishment. Conversely, once they have food in their stomach, shelter, security, and support, they will then be able to turn their eyes towards achievement.

Therapy can take several forms in Humanist Psychology, but the classic form is non-directing, "non-judgmental" listening in which the therapist hardly speaks at all, waiting for the clients to come to insights by themselves. Non-directive therapy is truly a miracle of modern medicine. Not because it works so well, but because they've convinced people to pay through the nose for the privilege of sitting in a room and solving their own problems.

In fairness to Humanist Psychologists, some prefer Gestalt therapy, in which role-playing is used to help patients reach understanding of their situation from a different perspective, as well as other therapy to add positive experiences to a patient's life in order to align their self-concept with their actual self.

Behaviorist

Behaviorist Psychology gets its start with a man called Ivan Pavlov, of whom most of you are already aware. Pavlov proved the power of mental association with physical action through his famous canine experiments. Every day when he presented food to his dogs, Pavlov would ring a bell and the food would make his dogs salivate in preparation for the meal. Eventually there didn't even have to be food present. Pavolov would ring his bell and the dogs would salivate. He is the pioneer of what we call classical conditioning.

B.F. Skinner is the other big name in Behaviorist Psychology. Using his famous "Skinner Boxes" he experimented on rats, rewarding them for some behaviors and punishing them for others. He described what we now call operant conditioning. If classical conditioning is behavior modification through association, operant conditioning is behavior modification through positive and negative reinforcement.

Behaviorist Psychology rejects introspective measures, restricting study and speculation to observable behavior reinforcement. It is in large degree based in modern scientific thought, concerning itself only with that which is observable, repeatable, and quantifiable. Consequently, research is of the utmost importance, as is pharmacology (giving medication), and tangible behavior modification.

Man is neither good nor bad. Man is a machine. He has a number of chemicals in his brain that make him feel certain ways at certain times. He is a habitual animal, and like all animals he can be trained. Inner turmoil is just another manifestation of that which is tangible and treatable. Treatment includes twelve step programs, medication, and carrot and stick measures.

Judeo-Christian

Judeo-Christian Psychology finds its basis in the Old and New Testaments of the Bible. It does not credit a particular Psychologist as its founder, rather it takes from other schools of Psychology and applies a Biblical worldview. It stresses the importance of the immortal soul, sin, God's relation to man, fidelity, forgiveness, and repentance.

Man was created to be good, but he is broken and in need of a Savior. This is why he does what he does not want to do and what he wants to do he does not. His fundamental problem is spiritual, and after that is addressed, mental issues may be better understood and treated. Contrary to many schools of thought, Judeo-Christian Psychology does not take for granted that all men want to be happy, rather most men desire destruction as evidenced by the self-sabotage and destruction of much of the population.

Limitations and freedom are not at odds, rather they are co-dependent. A man runs freely down a tall and narrow bridge when there are guardrails; he crawls on his hands and knees when the edges are open. Sin (wrong behavior or wrong motivation) creates further brokenness in individuals' lives as well as in the world as a whole. Turning from sin can bring relief and healing, but only acceptance of divine forgiveness can solve the spiritual issue from which all other problems originate.

"As a he thinketh in his heart, so is he" (from Proverbs 23:7, KJV). The focus, then, of Judeo-Christian Psychology is that of the heart, the core of a person. Everything flows from the heart, and so the heart is treated. Treatment can include counseling, meditation, prayer, and support groups.

Wait, What?

The last one may have thrown you off, but it is worth mentioning as an influential branch of therapy. All schools of Psychology have their roots in some kind of philosophy, and most kinds of philosophy have their roots in a religion. The argument can be made that Psychoanalytic Psychology springs from classical and pagan ideals, Humanistic Psychology from Buddhist ideals, Behaviorist Psychology from Atheism, and Judeo-Christian Psychology (obviously) from Judaism and Christianity. The world hasn't agreed as to what causes men to think and act how they do, and so it comes down to a clash of worldviews.

People have been asking "Why?" for a long time. Religion usually lies at the center of it somewhere when the question is asked. Reading Psychoanalytic Psychology, for example, you would think that you were reading the description of a religion if you didn't know any better. (And frankly, a bizarre religion) It all comes down to who, what, where, when, and ultimately, WHY.

As a writer, figure out what your perspective is and you will write better, with purpose and direction. It helps to know what you're saying when you try to say it. There is something to be learned from every branch of Psychology, but much of it is in opposition with other schools of thought. Do some research, figure out what makes sense, and you'll be a better writer for it.

The Bottom Line

If you know why people fear, you can scare them. If you know what makes them brave you can fill them with courage. If you know what they want, you can lead them pretty much anywhere. You probably think that I'm talking about what you should do to your audience. I'm not.

Do these things for your characters. Understand

people so that you'll know that a person who has been living on the street, starving, dodging the bullies is not necessarily going to wolf down a meal that's set in front of him even though he's hungry. Understand people so that your character's hesitation feels legitimate. Understand people so that we don't roll our eyes at your character's fear even though we don't share that particular fear. Remember, treat your characters like real people because they are real people. Then your audience will be affected. If your loyalty goes to your characters before your readers, then you will write compelling works that will move your readers anyway.

Finally, understand how people think so that you can avoid writing caricatures when you aren't like one of your characters. I've seen it on both ends of the spectrum: a writer who leans to the political left and thinks that all republicans are heartless monsters isn't going to write a very good republican character in a novel because he will reduce him to caricature. A writer who leans to the political right and thinks that all democrats are brainless monsters isn't going to write a very good democratic character. Perhaps Aaron Sorkin did it best in *The West Wing*, a TV drama set in the White House. Sorkin is not leaning to the left, he is sprinting towards it. And yet he understands the arguments of those who disagree with him, so it doesn't come off as cheap, regardless of whether or not you agree with him. Sorkin understands how people think, and he writes well because of it.

Can you write for a character nothing like you and do so with empathy and understanding, without endorsement?

Study how people think. Figure out what makes sense. Write better.

Exercises:

#1 Ponder the fundamental questions of Psychology: What is man's responsibility? Does he seek happiness? Are people fundamentally good or is it more complicated? What is perception? How does perspective shape our experience? What does it take for a person to be fulfilled? What is normal? What does it mean to have free will? Write these and any other pertinent big picture questions in a notebook and leave space to write what you come up with. Read before you write in any answers. Study what others have thought before you and judge for yourself.

#2 Read Psycho-Cybernetics by Dr. Maxwell Maltz, M.D., F.I.C.S. This is my favorite Psychology book, and it will make you think about these questions in a different light. More importantly, it offers a compelling answer to the question of "How do people think?" Don't skip the introduction.

#3 Be a student of people. Learn why they are the way that they are. It's probably under the surface, and it's probably more nuanced than you think. At the far side of the complexity, find simplicity and try to sum up your findings in your writing journal.

Chapter Nine: Framing Your Vision
creating the world in which you write

When I was in the first grade I was a big Hardy Boys fan.

I loved those books, couldn't get enough of them. I loved the mysteries, the characters, and the impossible situations that the crime-solving brothers always managed to get out of. I remember one night I was lying in bed reading *The Secret of Wildcat Swamp* or one of the other Hardy Boys books, and it was suddenly (and much too soon) time to go to sleep. I put my bookmark in the pages and closed it, my heart still racing from the adventure. I got down on my six year old knees, folded my hands, and prayed, "God, thank you for this day. Please help Chet and the Hardy boys get out of the room where they're-"

Wait.

The Hardy Boys are fictional characters, I remembered. I don't need to pray for their safety.

I felt a little stupid, but then I went to sleep and got over it.

The Realest, Fakest World in the World

It's amazing, isn't it? A book could draw me in so completely that I was worried for the characters and their situation as if it was really happening. When I was six years old, the world of the *Hardy Boys* felt like the real world. When I was eight the world of Narnia felt like the real world. When I was nine the world of *Lord of the Rings* felt like the real world. Today, people tell me that my books feel like the real world, no matter how fantastical the premise. As writers, we want to have a setting and a world that *enthralls* our reader, something believable and fantastic and wild that they can get lost in.

So how do we accomplish that? How can we build the realest, fakest world in the world?

It's called world building, and I'm going to teach you a few things to make you better at it. Let's get started.

A World By Any Other Name...

Let me start by saying that world building, though typically used in reference to speculative fiction, is a necessity regardless of genre. Isaac Asimov was certainly a world-builder, but so was Jane Austen. If you are writing literary fiction or epic battle fantasy, you still need to be able to build a setting that your audience believes long enough to get into the story and the characters. You need to have a coherent world for your characters to populate. (Be fruitful and multiply, characters! Hehe... - Ed.) It's getting late. My editor's getting silly.

What's in a world?

People, places, morals, an overarching tone, an overarching theme, history, and perspective.

This little list is a zip file for entire worlds. You unzip it by asking questions.

Let's use *Lord of the Rings* for our first example.

"Who are the villainous creatures of this world?" Well, they're called.... Orcs. They're sort of like goblins, but different. Lots of piercings. Green skin. Short. Mean. "Okay, where did the Orcs come from?" Well... they used to be elves. But Sauron twisted them and tortured them. He made them like dark versions of elves.

"Where does the action take place?" (For the answer to this one, I'm going to quote fantasy author Patrick Rothfuss, talking about his book *The Name of the Wind*)

"I think, 'He's going to need to spend some time in a really big city. Industrial revolution Londonish.' Where do big cities happen? At a confluence of trade routes. That's influenced by rivers. Where do rivers come from? There's aquifers and stuff. I ask these questions. I go, 'Why, why, why, why?'"[86]

What if we are to think about a book like *Brave New World*?

"What are the virtues and vices of this time and place in my story?" They've lost value for the individual. Values are oligarchic. Sexual ethics are non-existent. No, wait. They're existent, they're just the opposite of what we believe is appropriate. Society has lost its moral base, no longer even cognizant of the fact, except for one man whose inner turmoil turns to a desire for something better.

Do you see the power of this method of thinking? I've used examples from works you hopefully recognize, but the process can be the same with your book. This is where world building starts: asking questions.

When I'm working on a book concept and I don't have any notes to write down and I can't think of anything specific that should be in the story, I start writing down questions. "Where do they live?" "How do they feel about their neighbors?" "Do they have any siblings?" "What are people in their village afraid of?"

People are really good at answering questions.

Harness this ability. When you don't know where to start building, start asking questions. Ask others as well, but always answer the seven big questions I mentioned above: Who are the people in this world. What is this "world" like/what locations does it contain? What are the morals of the people I'm writing about? What is the feel and the tone of the world? (Hopeless and oppressive like in *The Hunger Games*? Fanciful and adventurous like in the *Hobbit*?) What is the overarching theme? (Obsession like in *Moby Dick*? The injustice of bad men who end up getting what they want like in Fitzgerald's *The Beautiful and the Damned*?) What is the history of this world? (Aslan breathed it into life in a great song of creation in the *Chronicles of Narnia*. In Zafo'n's *The Shadow of the Wind*, Barcelona is healing from the aftermath of the Spanish Civil War.) From what perspective do we see the events in this book? (From the eyes of the king, like in *The Once and Future King*? From the eyes of the street urchin like in *Mistborn*?) Perspective can be omnipotent, incidentally, and still be influenced by a certain character or bias. Who do we see the most of? Why is that?

You start with questions and you answer what you've asked. That is how you start building a world.

A Word of Caution

Wolfgang Amadeus Mozart was an anomaly.

A musical genius, he began composing symphonies as a small child. His father Leopold taught him from an early age, and he took to it as if he was born for the job. Throughout the course of his life he inspired, surprised, and awed his listeners with songs of such brilliant complexity forming a coherent and relatable whole. Wheels within wheels and cogs within cogs spin musically, rapturously, all working together in perfect harmony. The music can feel like an almost spiritual experience.

What manner of man must he have been to have held such beautiful intricacy inside of his mind? What worlds and oceans did he explore in his subconscious? How did he hold so many parts in his head at once?

I've heard people say these and similar things all of my life. I've heard people ask me how I can hold such a deep and complicated world as Pontus inside of my mind. I've heard people wonder how a man can rotate the universe in his mind like the great artists of history.

If you want to be a better writer, you need to understand why these questions are fundamentally flawed.

Mozart did not hold forty-seven parts in his head at once, and he certainly didn't blink a symphony into existence. My guess? He started with a trill on the piano, and he expanded it. Then he had a melody and he harmonized it. Then he had an idea for the horn section, and he crafted it. All the time, he's drawing little black notes on lined paper, chronicling his work.

Was Mozart a genius? Certainly. Should we be impressed and quieted by his work? Undoubtedly. Should we regard him as something more than human? No.

Every great work of intricacy and complexity begins with something small. Forty-seven parts did not spring into existence in Mozart's mind, Middle Earth did not spring into existence in Tolkien's mind, and Michelangelo did not sneeze and find the block in front of him to suddenly be *David*.

It started with a seed. That seed was watered with contemplation and it sprouted. Questions shot off in all directions in the form of leaves and branches, and they were pruned where necessary, bound up as they were going astray, and through it all, watered plentifully. The plant grew and grew and grew until it was a towering giant, flush with foliage and bark and levels upon levels upon levels.

It started with a seed. It started with a question.

Incidentally, one of the best ways to brainstorm for a new book idea is to take an accepted truth and imagine a world where it was the opposite. It sounds cheesy perhaps, but start reading books and watching movies and ask yourself if that isn't sort of what the writer did. Did you ever see the movie *Children of Men* with Clive Owen?

First of all, I'm impressed that you know Clive Owen to the degree that he would sit down and watch a movie with you. (Cheap joke – Ed.) Secondly, couldn't you have written a similar film by starting with the question, "What if people did *not* reproduce even though they really wanted to?"

What if cars drove people? What if most people were royalty and only a minority were peasants? What if people didn't die from lack of water, but from drinking it? What if water is a poison? Are people afraid of the ocean? What would life look like on a planet covered with seventy-five percent water? How did the oceans get poisoned in the first place? How did humanity survive, and what do they do now instead of drink water?

It's easy to write from a question, and it makes world building a manageable task instead of overwhelming. It makes it fun.

Personally...

The Weathermen started with a question. I asked myself what it would look like if all of the kookiest conspiracy theories were true. What if the government really was controlling people's opinions through subliminal messages on the TV? What if they really did control the weather?

Starfall started with a piece of poetry. I imagined stars falling to the earth like flakes of snow, so I wrote a poem about it. (Tragically, for the life of me I can't find it. It's been years and I think it's lost now.) The seed was very small, but I started asking questions. Why do stars fall? What happens if you see it happen? Do they fall here on earth or somewhere else? What is a star anyway?

This seed and these questions turned a piece of poetry a few lines long into a four hundred thousand word epic trilogy.

You will have to know far more about your world than what goes in your book in order to write it well (Remember, write from a place of abundance). Again, to reference Rothfuss, he says that for most writers you should include in your book about ten percent of what you know about the world you created. In his case, he says it's more like four because world building is his hobby and passion.[37]

Every decision you make and every question you answer will inform your writing, even if it's implicit.

Be a Sculptor

World building is like carving a sculpture: remove everything that isn't like an elephant. (That was too obscure of a reference. No one's going to get it. – Ed.)

I'm just kidding. Really, though, world building is a lot like sculpting.

Imagine you have a giant block of blank marble in front of you. Your job is to carve it into the likeness of the protagonist in *Simeon Volcano*, the intrepid fire-breathing monkey trainer cracking his whip. (Stop it. – Ed.) Can you do something so complicated with one stroke of the chisel? Are you going to walk around the block, pick the perfect place to strike, and voila?

No, of course not. You are going to make a move, then refine based off of that choice. You make a move, then you refine. You refine and you refine and you refine until your vision is complete- probably the vision has improved as you worked. Just like the statue is somewhere inside of that blank piece of stone, your world is somewhere "inside" of you. It just takes a bit of refining to get it out.

Start with a seed. Ask yourself questions. Don't forget to marvel at what unfolds.

Exercises:

#1   In your writing journal, write "Book Ideas" at the top. Then, underneath, list as many questions as you can think of in the form of, "In the real world it's like this, but what if..." Write down at least ten. Which ones get you excited?

#2   Pick one or two of the questions from the first exercise and write it at the top of another page. What other questions does it make you ask? Write them down. If you start thinking of answers, start jotting those down too. If you really like where this is going, get a dedicated notebook for the story idea and start world building.

#3   Pick your favorite book and write down the answers to the Big Seven I alluded to earlier in the chapter. Who are the people? Where does this take place/what is it like there? What are the morals of the people in this book? What is the tone? What is the overarching theme? What sort of history is there? What perspective do we see it from?

#4   Set a timer for twenty minutes. Write a story about a woman named Joy. She's nervous about her first date with someone named Daryl that her friend Sandra set her up with. The doorbell rings, and there he is. Off to the restaurant. What happens? Once you're finished, set the timer again for twenty minutes. Write the exact same story but through the perspective of the guy taking her out. When you're done, read both versions and see what you discover about perspective and how it influences your writing.

Chapter Ten: Speako dee Englush?
fluency and the tools of the trade

Earlier this year I was on my way to Utah for a friend's wedding. I was traveling with my best friend, the aforementioned mountain man Preston, and we were having a great time joking and laughing in the airport waiting for our plane to arrive. As airports are wont to do, they changed our gate and announced it over the loudspeaker, so we shrugged, picked up our things and began to walk away. I noticed one gentleman, however, was not getting up. I had heard him speaking on the phone in Spanish earlier, and I wondered if he had understood the announcement. I politely asked him in Spanish if he had heard the gate reassignment and he told me that he hadn't. I told him to follow us, and he was very grateful.

His name was Jonathan, and he didn't really speak any English, but that was fine because we were speaking in his language. We talked about everything as we sat at our new gate: politics, religion, geography, life stories. We were all over the map and having a great time conversing. Then, without warning, a crippling fear seized my chest:

What if I don't speak Spanish???

Laugh if you want, but it was actually sort of terrifying for a moment. I didn't want to look like an idiot or not understand what the poor guy was saying.

Then I remembered that having a fluid forty-five minute conversation with a native speaker from the South of Mexico was probably not a fluke and that I had been studying and speaking Spanish for ten years.

Silly, right? I got over it and we had a nice conversation.

Here's to Looking at You

Talking about fluency when we're discussing a foreign language is all well and good, but rarely do we ask ourselves how fluent we are in our own native tongue. English is a large, dynamic, and versatile language with approximately 1,025,109.8 words, according to the Global Language Monitor in 2014. How do you end up with .8 of a word you ask? I have no idea. Oxford Dictionary claims that if you count regional words and archaic words, there are probably about three quarters of a million words in the English language. Merriam-Webster agrees that the number of English words is probably between 750,000 and 1,000,000.

The bottom line? There are an absurd number of words in this tongue of ours. There are innumerable ways of describing any given event, concept, or thing. If we only know one or two ways, we are severely limiting ourselves as writers.

What is writing anyway? It is the magical transference of thought and sensation into words that will evoke the same or similar thoughts and sensations in the mind of the reader. Isn't that an easier job with more words at our disposal? Otherwise we are like the archer who marched into battle unaware that he only had one arrow in his quiver. Once that was gone, well... He had a bad time. (Stop using jokes that no one is going to get. −Ed.)

Le Mot Juste

"Shortly" and "directly" are synonyms, right? You can say, "I'll be there shortly," or "I'll be there directly," and we would say that you are expressing the same idea. This is true, and yet it's as inexact as saying that lilac and lavender are both purple. We are artists and words are our paint. Let's have the integrity to understand shades and tones of the different terms we employ.

Shortly means soon and directly means soon, but really, shortly is less urgent than directly. Their *denotation* is the same. They both mean anon. (Easy, Shakespeare. –Ed.) I just wanted to say "anon." It means soon. Their *connotation*, however, is different. Shortly means in the future, probably after I finish whatever it is I'm currently doing. Directly means *now*, as soon as humanly possible. No obstacles will stand in my way; I'm coming.

Don't say shortly when you mean directly. Don't paint with lilac when you want lavender, or mauve, or deep purple. I find that Deep Purple works best when painting smoke on the water, but that's another story entirely. (I told you to stop making jokes no one is going to get! – Ed.)

The French have a term for using the perfect word at the perfect time in the perfect place. They call it "Le mot juste." As writers, how can we find le mot juste if we don't know that many words?

Yes, sometimes people go out of their way in order to... Well, actually sometimes people run screaming, flailing their arms and sprinting out of their way in order to use "big words." Perhaps C.S. Lewis' quote is appropriate here:

"Don't use words too big for the subject. Don't say 'infinitely' when you mean 'very'; otherwise you'll have no word left when you want to talk about something really infinite."[87]

I'm not talking about forcing it, but being able to use the word "torpor" instead of "sluggishness" can make a big difference. "Sloth" instead of "laziness," "trials" instead of "hard times," "crimson" instead of "red," "antidisestablishmentarianism" instead of "the idea that removing the Church of England from its political thews would be a mistake." (Now you're just showing off. – Ed.)

Some concepts are even difficult to describe unless you know the word for it. It isn't easy to come up with a stand-in for the word "rapport" for example. It is a concept that is difficult to reduce to a more common word, and yet what a concept! You cannot write about it if you don't know about it.

The moral of the story is this: learn more words. Even if you think you have an impressive vocabulary, a few more arrows in your quiver can't hurt if you use them judiciously.

Well, I suppose the point of arrows sort of is to hurt. The fletching not so much. (Stop it with the puns. – Ed.)

Other Areas of Fluency

Fluency as a writer means more than buffing up your lexicon, though that is extremely important. Being able to write with nuance on the history or culture of a particular time and place relevant to your story is key. Being able to draw parallels between events in your book and real life events is helpful. Being able to properly imitate a dialect or speech pattern will make you a better writer as well. Yes, these have to do with research, but you will have to do less research in the future if you are better educated now. Educate yourself into fluency and write from abundance.

Let me give you an example of two books, both by great authors, one more successful than the other, both having to do with imitating a speech pattern unlike their own.

The Magic Help

Orson Scott Card, one of my favorite authors from childhood and an enduring example of fine writing in the sci-fi and fantasy genres, once wrote a book called *Magic Street*. It was basically a modern day, surrealist interpretation of Shakespeare's *A Midsummer Night's Dream*. Kathryn Stockett, who worked in magazine publishing prior to the publication of her debut novel, wrote a book called *The Help*, which many of you will be familiar with because of the movie, if not because of the book itself. It is about the plight of African-American maids in the Deep South, pre-civil rights.

What on earth do these two novels have in common, you ask? It's probably not what you would expect. Both are examples of a white author writing with a black voice.

Orson Scott Card is a tremendous author, and I've sung his praises more than once in this book, but in this particular instance we didn't see his best work. It was an interesting idea, but it ultimately was not his best, in a large part because the voice was not fluid. It sounded like an older white guy trying to write for a young black kid. It was an older white guy writing for a young black kid.

Stockett's book, however, was a smashing success. She stood in the shoes of the various characters of her book brilliantly. When the maids were speaking, it was as if a maid had dictated the lines to her. It was fluid, it was believable, and it hooked the reader in.

Stockett has only written one novel as far as I'm aware at this point in time. Card has written dozens and dozens of them, and quite well. I don't think that I overstep my bounds to call Card the superior author- and yet in this case, Stockett's work comes out on top because the voices were fluid and believable. The voices were fluid and believable because of Stockett's fluency with the relevant dialects.

Oh, incidentally *The Help* has sold well over ten million copies and spent more than one hundred weeks on the New York Times Bestseller list. You've never heard of *Magic Street*, have you?

The Cowboy Scholar

If anyone ever starts to call Louis L'Amour "The Cowboy Scholar" I want credit because I just made it up. Feel free to quote me on that, and mail me a quarter every time you do. (In your dreams. – Ed.)

I've talked about the great American Western writer Louis L'Amour already in this book, but to refresh your memory, he was a great American Western writer. He wrote a book unlike most of his works called *The Education of a Wandering Man* that thankfully, I had the good fortune to read early on in my own education. Pick up a copy if you ever get the chance. The book itself is very insightful and interesting and a great encouragement to your life as a writer. However, I'm going to talk about what's in the back of the book, after the story is through.

Louis L'Amour had a habit of keeping track of what books he read every year. He would keep lists so that he could go back and look over what he had read and remember what it was he spent so much time mulling over. He read poetry, philosophy, classics, contemporary novels, diaries, journals, scientific works, and much else. More impressive perhaps than simply the variety of his reading was the volume. In a typical year he would read more than a hundred books. He was always seeking to better understand what he was writing about and learning about. He was never afraid to track down an expert and ask them questions. I defy you to pick up any one of the over one hundred books that The Cowboy Scholar (it has a ring to it, right?) wrote during his lifetime and find a single instance where it does not seem like he is an expert.

He writes with fluency, both of language and of subject matter. He went out of his way to learn how to do so.

Multi-Lingual or Multi-Pringle?

(I'm going to butt in here before you start and just let out a long sigh due to the incredible hokiness of your chapter title. Ugggggggggghhhhhhhhhh. I wonder if it's too late to get into accounting. – Ed.)

Pay no attention to my editor. He's kind of a Debbie Downer.

In the past, the acquisition and learned fluency of foreign languages was considered primary in the foundation of proper education. Today, sadly, it is not. With the status of our native language of English as lingua franca (which is of course, French for "the

French language") we have allowed ourselves an unhelpful laxity toward understanding language.

I can tell you from my own experience, and many others will tell you the same, that you will understand your own language better if you learn another one. You don't understand sleep when you're asleep but when you're awake. You don't understand drunkenness until you're sober.[38] And you don't understand how warm it is in your climate-controlled cabin until you take a step into the frigid air outside. Learning another language opens your eyes to the fact that the way English is set up is not how thought has to be expressed. Many languages have a concept of gendered nouns. That isn't something we really come across in English, but it makes you look at things differently. In Latin not only are verbs conjugated, but nouns are *declined*. (Care for a noun? No thank you.) That means that nouns are modified according to their usage in a sentence. We don't have anything like that, but once you understand a different system, you begin to see the structure of our own tongue. You can interact with the particular character of English. French is romantic, and it will teach you how to speak romantically in your own tongue. Spanish is passionate, and it will put fire in your voice. Latin is stern, and it will make your descriptions efficient.[40]

Is it a requirement to speak more than one language to be a good writer in your own tongue? Probably not. Will it help you to that end? Yes. Learning to express thought through a different lens will make you better at doing it.

Personally, I speak English, Spanish, a good deal of French, and some Latin. I have also studied some Greek and German, though I would not claim to speak either of those last two at this point because one of you might come up to me at a conference and try to have a conversation with me. I'm sweating already. WHAT IF I DON'T SPEAK SPANISH??

Kidding. Just ask Jonathan if I speak Spanish. He'll back me up.

In all seriousness, it is a goal of mine to be fluent in five languages. With discipline and practice, this is absolutely an attainable goal. Does it have to be yours? No. And yet I would recommend trying to learn a second language if you don't know one. If you had the good fortune of being raised in a bilingual home, consider adding a third. It will make you more versatile and better at the magical process of turning thoughts and sensations into words that will be received as the same thoughts and sensations that you intended. Don't just sit on the couch eating chips and assume that your current understanding of language is the best it can possibly be. (There's the justification for the pun. Right in the nick of time.)

Saying More With Less

There is an often repeated story (that actually isn't true[41], but the point of it remains) that says Ernest Hemingway was once challenged to write a compelling story in the space of one line of newsprint. His response was six words and chilling.

For Sale: baby shoes. Never worn.

Stop and think about that for a moment. Read it again.

What a story, huh? You can just feel the heartbreak of the father who dictated these words to the clerk at the newspaper office, see his heartbroken wife weeping into his shoulder. So many hopes and dreams crushed in a billow of misfortune: a child that never was, the tragedy of miscarriage.

Some occasions call for verbosity. Others call for brevity.

Be capable of being powerfully brief.

The Point

Be able to say things a lot of different ways. Understand a lot of different perspectives. You don't have to agree with these perspectives- in fact, if you agree with every perspective you come across I guarantee you're doing something wrong- but understand them. How many good idioms do you know?

Study English. Don't assume yourself to be its master because "dada" was your first word instead of *"Le fromage, s'il vous plaît."* You can say, "Boys don't want to date Cindy," or you can say, "Cindy? The *tide* wouldn't take her out." It depends on the circumstance which will be the better fit, but you ought to want to be versatile, as we've discussed previously.

Read a lot. Stop reading and look up whatever words you come across that you don't know, or jot them down on a pad of paper to look up once you're done with the chapter. When speaking with others, ask them what they mean by a term you've never heard, don't just nod your head and pretend that you understand. Learning takes humility, but it is abundantly worth the effort. The smartest man is the one who is willing to look stupid if it means understanding. I have tremendous respect for someone who doesn't think twice about asking for clarification when he does not understand.

John Donne was a master of the English language. Robert Frost was a master of the English language. F. Scott Fitzgerald was a master of the English language. Shakespeare was a master of the English language. At present, no offense, I'm going to withhold your name from the list. That doesn't mean that you aren't a good writer, it means that you have a ways to go, and so do I. Let's be humble enough to admit that, and then let's do something about it.

Let's pursue fluency.

Exercises:

#1   Choose three letters of the alphabet. Write them at the top of a sheet of paper. Then, write a letter to a fictional pen pal (or a real pen pal if you want) using only words that begin with one of those three letters. Was it hard? Try it again with a different three letters. For added challenge, ask someone else to pick the letters for you and see if you can do it. Grab a writing buddy and choose the same three letters, then see whose resulting epistle is superior. Have fun with it- and yes, I have done this and yes, it is possible.

#2   Write a six word story. Do it several times. Pick out your favorite and analyze why it was better than the others. How does it stack up against Hemingway's? How could it be better? Show it to somebody and get some feedback.

#3   Write a poem in which every word is a minimum of five letters long. No exceptions.

#4   Be able to destroy your friends at scrabble.

#5   Pick a goal number of books that you would like to read this year and keep track.

#6   Sign up for a word of the day app or get a word of the day calendar.

#7   Consider learning another language, particularly Latin, Greek, Spanish, French, or German as they will be helpful in helping you understand where English came from. Duolingo.com is a great free resource to get you started.

#8 Make a point to incorporate new words you learn into conversation at least a couple of times so that you remember them.

Chapter Eleven: Breathing In
learning to be inspired constantly

Writers, and really all artists, talk a lot about the concept of inspiration: that magical, intangible elixir of creative power that comes upon us without warning and allows us to write. When someone is sitting around, unmotivated and unproductive, they say, "I just don't have any inspiration..." And then we all nod our heads knowingly and let them off the hook. After all, the poor guy doesn't have any inspiration, right? We all know what that's like. Nothing he can do about it. Right?

Do you know what the word inspiration actually, literally means? In a strict sense, it means breathing in, taking a breath.[42] If you aren't experiencing inspiration, you'll soon be experiencing expiration and you will be mourned in isolation for never reaching your aspiration. Vacation. Fermentation. I can do this all day. Celebration. (Stop stop stop stop stop. – Ed.)

If you aren't breathing you're dying, and unless someone is reading this to you while you're hooked up to an iron lung, you're breathing. You don't have a shortage of inspiration, you just need to know how to use it. That is what I'm going to show you in this chapter: the beginning of learning how to be an artist who can take inspiration from anything and then produce beautiful works.

Clouds and Ink Blots

In 1921 with the publication of *Psychodiagnostik*, a

common psychological evaluation known as the ink blot test or the Rorshach test was invented by Hermann Rorshach. You've probably heard of it or seen a variation of it at some point in your life. The test has become almost synonymous with psychological therapy in the collective mind of popular culture. The graphic novel *The Watchmen* even has a superhero named Rorshach with a large inkblot across his mask.

What the Rorshach test is, essentially, is a series of ten symmetrical but otherwise completely random blots of ink on cards. The psychologist presents one card, asks the patient what it looks like, then goes, "Hmm... Very interesting," and writes down his response before moving onto the next card.

Why does this test work? Why are people, even very mentally challenged people, able to look at a random blot without inherent meaning and imagine it is a particular form? It's the same reason that lovers are able to lie on their backs in the park pointing at clouds and saying, "That one's a dog! That one looks like my third grade teacher Mrs. Rosenbloom. Look! A potato." There is no dog, no Mrs. Rosenbloom, and as we all know, no potato. They are clouds. And yet the human mind is so dazzlingly creative that even with the most modest of exertions it can see a cast of characters in the ice particles floating overhead.

When You Don't Know What to Write...

You are far more creative than you realize. We are going to talk about specific ways of taking inspiration shortly (notice I didn't say directly), but first, it bears mentioning that a great way of getting back into the game when you don't know what to write is simply free association.

Free association is when you write whatever comes to mind in that moment. Take a blank sheet of paper, and even if you haven't got the foggiest notion of what to write, just put the pen on the paper and start shaping the ink into words. Write a line of dialog. Describe something. Write something provocative like:

"She's dead."
"I bet the fire-breathing monkeys did it."
"No, Gaston, you're wrong. It was their trainer. Their trainer is the one who breathes fire..."

And then boom! You're writing a story. Write whatever comes to mind and then shape it. Let the creative juices of your soul pour out and shape them as they spill. We're not talking about a final draft here; we're talking about a way to unclog your creative mechanism. Maybe what comes out is mostly drivel, but there was an interesting term you used at one point. It was surprising, and it makes you think. Ponder it. How can you write about it or incorporate it appropriately in a story?

Maybe most of what you wrote is silly, but you have a character name suddenly. Run with it. "Gaston... who is Gaston? He solves crimes, definitely. He never wanted to though. He comes from a long line of detectives in his family and he always wanted to rebel, break the mold. It looked like he was going to do it too, disappointing his father and everyone by living for himself and becoming a doctor. But when his father was murdered under suspicious circumstances, he was roped in, forced to use the training his father had embedded in him all his life in order to solve the murder. He doesn't want to do it, but now it's personal. Luckily, he's the best detective there ever was."

See? I just made that up right now. Not a bad character. And what a silly beginning to draw that from! But who cares? No one sees my writing exercises anyway unless I write a book, include them, and publish it for the world to see.

At any rate, maybe we'll see the adventures of Gaston again someday... (Over my dead body. – Ed.) What my editor clearly doesn't realize is that if we find his dead body we'll need Gaston to solve the murder. (Dang it. – Ed.) Victory is mine, editor. Victory is mine.

And *Another* Thing!

Another extremely powerful way of getting past the feeling of having no inspiration is the rant.

"The rant?" you say. "The incredible creature of science produced in a cataclysmic laboratory accident? Half rhino, half ant??"

Well, no, not that. That has never been a thing. Pipe down and listen.

You are passionate about something. You are angry about something. There is at least one thing in this big wide world that really, really pisses you off. When people bring it up your heart rate increases, your speech quickens, and everyone is sort of hoping that you'll shut up at some point in the future.

If you can rant about it you can write about it. Injustice elicits a tremendous flow of words from most of us. Make showing that injustice, righting that wrong, healing that wound your purpose. Get a piece of paper and rant to your heart's content. Then, when you're finished, look over it and ask yourself how you could demonstrate these things in a book.

Your gears are already spinning, aren't they?

A word of caution: don't sermonize. If it's too on the nose, like some of the awful, awful, dare I say it? AWFUL scripts I've had to read then your point won't be made very well. There is by necessity a certain amount of subtlety in effective writing. However, figuring out what you are passionate about and what you can rant about gives you the skeleton of a purpose. As you will recall from the first chapter of this fine, fine book (Oh, so humble. – Ed.), if you have a great purpose you are on the road to writing a great book. From there a clear path exists. Only don't sacrifice the quality of plot and the depth of characters for the sake of sermonizing. Let it inform your work, not crush it under its iron heel.

Also, make sure that your rant is not an outlet for you to stew in your own bitterness. You can probably write from that place, it just won't necessarily be the best thing for your soul, in my opinion. Just a thought. Rants about injustice toward others are usually more interesting anyway.

Rant and the world rolls their eyes. Rant privately, figure out how to incorporate that rant into an intriguing story, and the world leans forward to listen. Also, you've now solved your inspiration problem.

Ignorance is Lit

Never underestimate the power of wondering. If you don't know what to write about, pick something you don't understand and make up a fanciful answer.

Rudyard Kipling, the famed author of *The Jungle Book*, *Kim*, and others, wrote a book called *Just So Stories*. They are little vignettes that answer childish questions such as, "How did the leopard get his spots?" and "Why are elephants so big?" Rudyard didn't know how the heck leopards got their spots, so he made up a funny little story with all of the animals in the jungle. You can do the same thing. Don't be afraid to feel like you're starting off with a little folklore. "Where does all the water go when I pour it down the sink?" Show us how the water doesn't go underground or back into the ocean or any such nonsense as that. Show us that it's actually disappearing! An evil underground villain has co-opted all of the drains in the world and is stealing our water!

What a lame starting question, right? And yet you could absolutely write a good children's story off of the response. Would it be an Alex Cross murder mystery? Probably not, unless James Patterson happens to be reading this book and decides to use it in his next novel. Hi James!

It doesn't have to be silly, either. "Just so" stories do tend to be children's fiction, but not always. Think of something like *Neverwhere* by Neil Gaimon, where he wonders about the lives of the forgotten people in the city- the hobos, the drug addicts, the prostitutes. Where do they go every night? What happens to them?

He didn't really know, so he made up an answer and got a very original, fun novel out of it. (Yes, I know that he wrote it as a tv series originally. He wrote the novel afterwards. Same deal. Go away.)

Magical realism thrives off of "just so" stories and questions, as does children's literature, as does fantasy, occasionally. Even science fiction. If you are feeling uninspired, pick something, anything, that you don't understand and explain it fancifully.

Everything is a Place to Start

What defines you? What happened to you as a child? What are you afraid of? What are you proud of? What do you do to forget about your problems? Where is your favorite spot in the world? What would your perfect vision of society look like? Who hurt you? What does forgiveness mean to you? How could things be better? What is different about you? Who is the most interesting person you've ever known? What have you always wanted to do but were never able?

Write about it. Write about it, write about it, write about it, write about it.

Everything is inspiration. It is the air you breathe! Connect the dots on the floor of the bathroom tile. Look at the clouds and see raging battles between lions and elves. Look into your soul and consider the hero you always hoped to become. Read history and ponder how it could have been different.

You are drowning in an ocean of inspiration. Stop flailing your arms, take a deep breath, and swim. Everything is inspiration. Everything is a place to start. Writing is art and art is sub-creation and you LIVE IN CREATION.

I don't want this to come off like I'm chastising you- rather the opposite. I hope to encourage you. If you've felt like you don't have a leg to stand on creatively or that you used to have good ideas but now you just can't think of anything, remember that every time you breathe air into your lungs it is inspiration. Exhale a creative work. It takes focus and a good bit of effort, but the possibilities are endless, rich, and at the tip of your fingers continuously.

To once more quote the esteemed artist Twyla Tharp:

"Creativity is more about taking the facts, fictions, and feelings we store away and finding new ways to connect them. What we're talking about here is metaphor. Metaphor is the lifeblood of all art, if it is not art itself. Metaphor is our vocabulary for connecting what we are experiencing now with what we have experienced before. It's not only how we express what we remember, it's how we interpret it- for ourselves and others."

It's Been Done Before

Finally I want to talk about one of the most crushing wet blanket lies that will ever assail you as a writer.

"It's been done before."

"Oh, man... I had a great idea for a book where a Nicaraguan drug lord ends up in CIA custody and turns, working against the drug moguls now from the inside! I was really excited about it, but I realized that double agent novels have been written a lot of times, so I guess I can't write it..."

NO! It isn't true that something like that disqualifies you from writing or compromises your idea. You say it's been done before? Well, you're right. It has been done before. So has everything else.

We're up against roughly six thousand years of recorded human history, folks. The oldest thing we can reliably call a novel is probably *The Epic of Gilgamesh* (read it, if you haven't) and that's easily five thousand years old! And before that there was mythology! Literally billions of people have written, dreamed, and plotted narrative before you were ever even a twinkle in your daddy's eye. ("Mom, where do babies come from?" "Twinkles, sweetheart. They come from twinkles.")

The hard truth is this: it's been done before.

And yet it has never been done by you.

No one has ever lived who was exactly like you. No one has ever had the exact same experiences you've had, knew exactly the same set of people, or talked in exactly the same way. It is worth doing because you've never done it before. If "it's been done before" is a reason to give up, then you might as well stay in bed for the rest of your life and never do anything.

Thankfully, it isn't a reason to give up. Make it your own. Write from your heart. Let your emotions, thoughts, visions, convictions, dreams, and desires shape the work, and it will be something new.

Sub-Creation

Art is twofold: structure and breath. If we look at the first creativity, the grand act of creation, what do we see? In the book of Genesis (chapter 2 verse 7, NIV), it says:

> *"Then the LORD God formed a man from the dust of the ground and breathed into his nostrils the breath of life, and the man became a living being."*

We've talked about structure already in the first half of this book. We've talked about inspiration in this chapter. If you want to create brilliant works of art, whether you are a painter, a dancer, a playwright, a craftsman, a novelist, or a cinematographer, understand this principle: form the structure, then put a little piece of yourself in it. Breathe into your work and make it come alive in this, the grand act of imitation of the first creation. Writing is sub-creation, so take inspiration from the first inspiration, which was breathed into us. Shape and mold, then put yourself into your art.

That is how to make something brilliant.

Exercises:

#1   In your writing journal, tape a picture to the left side of the page and stare at it for a while. Then write. Write from that picture; let it be your inspiration.

#2   Pick up a dictionary and flip to a random word. Write it and its definition at the top of a page in your writing journal. Then write from that word; let it be your inspiration. See what happens.

#3   Hit shuffle on your music and listen to the first song that comes up one time through in its entirety. Then, set a timer for the length of the song and write. Let the music be your inspiration. If you like where it's going and you don't have enough time to finish, keep writing.

#4   Write from a smell. Get creative. Sniff your shampoo bottle or your deodorant or your lunch or a flower outside and write straightaway based off of that sensation. Where does it lead you creatively?

#5   Think of a memory from your childhood. Hold that memory in your mind as you write in your journal a piece of fiction. It can be directly or indirectly related, but write something else while keeping in mind that memory to see how it influences your creative decisions.

#6   Think of what you tend to rant about. Write down possible book ideas that would allow you to rant.

#7   Read *The Epic of Gilgamesh*. It's short and it may well be the oldest thing we can get away with calling a novel. Think about how storytelling has changed and how it hasn't.

Chapter Twelve:
The Tremendous Responsibility of the Artist

Fair warning: it's going to get real for a moment, but I promise there is a light at the end of the darkness. I joke a lot in this book, but the following is not a joke, and unfortunately very real.

In 2009 a 17 year old named Andrew Conley choked his 10 year old brother to death with his hands. He slammed his head into the ground repeatedly, held the choke about twenty minutes, then tied two plastic bags around his head when he was done to make sure that he wouldn't wake up. He then dumped the body in a park.[43] It wasn't an accident; it was very much on purpose.

During the first hour of his interrogation, once it was determined what he had done, he said this to the police: "I don't know if you've heard of it, but it's called 'Dexter,' and it's on Showtime. And I feel like him because he's a serial killer of bad people... but I just feel like him." Speaking of the murderer, prosecutor Negangard told reporters this in 2011, "He told us he was reading books about it- on serial killers. He was watching 'Dexter.'"

For those of you unfamiliar with the show, 'Dexter' is a television series about a psychopath named, obviously, Dexter. In the show, his dad sees certain traits in his son and concludes that he is going to grow up to be a serial killer. So what does he do? He trains him how not to get caught and to only commit mass murder on "bad" people. There's a lot of sneaking around, pretending to live a normal life working for the police department, holding normal relationships, and so on, all the while Dexter is murdering people he thinks deserve it because he likes killing and he feels like he has to kill *someone*.

After the murderer I mentioned a moment ago, I won't say his name a second time, killed his brother, he drove to his girlfriend's house and gave her a promise ring. His brother was in the trunk of his car at the time. It was exactly the sort of scenario you could find on the show: pretending everything is fine while there's a body under the whatever.

The murderer began fantasizing about killing around the time the show began to air.

I wish I could say that this was an isolated incident, but it was not. I have read several similar news stories of other first-time murderers obsessed with *Dexter*.[44]

A Significantly More Hopeful Example

In 1946 Superman fought the Ku Klux Klan.

It happened as a series of radio show episodes titled, *Superman versus the Men of Hate*. Troubled by the resurgence and reappearance of the Klan in the South in response to civil rights efforts, Superman's creators Jerry Siegel and Joe Shuster decided to do what they could to combat the prejudice, violence, and deplorability of the Klan. They decided to make Superman fight an organization very, very similar to the Klan. Basically, Superman has a friend with dark skin and prejudiced evil men try to do him harm. Without getting into the whole plot, Superman fought the "Men of Hate" (the KKK without calling it the KKK) and won on national radio.

Children across the country, and specifically in the South, sat on the floor listening to Superman line up against the bad guys who would dare to be part of something so stupid as prejudicial violence against people of other races. Often these children sat listening to these programs unaware that their father had a white sheet and hood hanging up in his closet.

What do you think happened? Kids across the country ran around their front yards pretending to be Superman. And who was the villain they valiantly fought against? You guessed it: the white-sheeted men of hate.

The Klan didn't disappear overnight, but the radio broadcast helped the generation that was to come develop an early disgust for the organization. The Klan never recovered its strength or size after the mid-sixties, which was right about the time those kids who grew up listening to Superman on the radio might have been joining up. They didn't.

The Meaning of All This

"How many a man has dated a new era in his life from the reading of a book?"[45]
– Henry David Thoreau

What is a story? We talk so much about how to craft narratives in writing, how to describe a situation better, and what does or doesn't work for the reader, but rarely do we ever take a step back and look at the big picture. What is storytelling? How should we think about it? What happens to a person when they hear a story, read a good book, see a movie?

We can get so lost in the details sometimes that we forget why we're doing this in the first place.

So what is a story? It's a metaphor for life. Remember that Twyla Tharp quote in the last chapter? It's absolutely true. Art is metaphor, and metaphor leads us back to life. Art teaches us how to look at the world, and for the stories that impact us, we believe what they say. Narrative drives culture.

It can be subtle; it can be extreme. Many are the books and films with subtle messages of goodness and hope. Many are the same with subtle messages of crime paying off, infidelity making you cool, revenge justifiable. And then there are shows and books that flat-out glorify serial killers.

What does your story glorify? What does it hold up as heroic and good? Good things? Or questionable things?

It isn't Sunday morning, this certainly isn't church, but you as a writer are absolutely a preacher. Anyone who gets to talk to someone for hours at a time (like when someone reads your book) is preaching a message intentionally or not. Whether you meant to instill a moral in your story or not, it has one. Is it a good moral? Is it a message that benefits society?

These are hard questions, but all joking aside, they are terribly necessary. Ask yourself before you write, "Is my book going to be edifying?"

The Takeaway of a Short Chapter

I hope I haven't caught you totally off-guard with this, but it is truly so important. For some reason when so many people begin writing, they take it as a necessity to be "edgy." Be edgy, fine. Be dark if the situation calls for it- I'm not saying everything has to be sunshine and rainbows- but don't be detrimental. Don't write a book that is going to harm the society that receives it.

Why? Because you're better than moral compromise, and your position as culture-maker imbues you with a certain responsibility. A good faith effort to be edifying is all any of us can do, so don't lay up nights worrying that someone might misinterpret what you said or want to be like the villain in your book. There is a tremendous difference between writing a convincing, evil villain and making the villain the hero. Your book is probably glorifying something. What is it? It's worth considering.

This is a message that I give every time a writer comes to me for advice. I urge you to remember it and do the same. If there's one thing you take from this book, let it be this: write from a place of good purpose. Purpose should drive our work for so many reasons- it allows us to have vision for our characters, innovative plot ideas, it informs our language, and so much more. It also allows us to write in a way that helps those we entertain and inform.

My charge to you is don't write on accident. Don't write haphazardly. Write with purpose. Write from a place of abundance.

Do those things, and you will have done your job well. I'm proud of you.

What are you waiting for? There are blank pages to be tamed, notebooks to be filled. The world is your oyster, and here is your knife. Pry that sucker open.

Maybe there's a pearl inside.

Exercises:

#1   Sit and ponder.

#2   Figure out objectively what the moral takeaways have been in your previous works. How can future works be better?

#3   Start writing and never fear the blank page again.

What's Next?

Congratulations! You've made it through the book. Now, there are three things that I hope you'll consider doing:

1. **Write an Amazon review of this book**

   This is incredibly helpful when readers take just a minute out of there day to share with potential readers online what they thought of the book. Leaving reviews helps others figure out what a book is about and if it's good- from an unbiased source (you). It helps me out a lot, and readers benefit as well. Everyone wins! Go to amazon.com right now and leave a review.

2. **Consider signing up for a *Writing With Purpose* workshop**.

   In only one intensive writing session with author W.A. Fulkerson (me), your creative world will be turned upside down in the best possible way. Five different workshops offer everything you might need to kick-start, restart, or accelerate your writing! Don't miss out! Go to www.wafulkerson.com for more details.

3. **Tell your friends and family about this book.**

   Let's spread the secrets of better writing to the world! If you know someone who could benefit from reading this book, mention it in conversation or offer to lend them your copy. We have seen depressed writers reinvigorated and encouraged after experiencing *Writing With Purpose*, and we want to reach as many people as possible.

Thanks, and happy writing!   -W.

Acknowledgments

Some books are a long time in the making, others come quickly and relatively painlessly. Thankfully, this book was the latter. I have a passion for excellent writing, and over the years I had collected a lot of ideas for teaching it. When it came time to create this book, I had a wealth of information at my disposal (writing from abundance). So as always, I would like to acknowledge God first, who made me to write. After that I have to thank my dad, Jeff Fulkerson, who bugged me to write a book on writing for at least a year. Finally I gave in, and I'm glad that I did.

To the rest of my family, mom, Trevor, Jeff, and Emily, thank you for your unending support and your penchant for finding typos that everyone else has missed. It's an honor that all of you always read my books and give feedback, and I am very grateful.

Thanks to Perennial Press, Marwan Hasoon, my focus group members who served as guinea pigs for much of the material in this book and for the accompanying workshops. It's exciting to see so many like-minded individuals reinvigorated to write.

Thank you to Justin Sobaje, Brian, Levi, Zac, Chris, and David. Thank you to Azusa Pacific University, which is not my alma mater, but my host for much of the writing of this book. Between a chair inside of Marshburn Library facing the orchid tree outside its windows and a desk in Darling Library facing the fountain, the vast majority of this book was written.

I'd like to thank the love of my life. Rita, your support, encouragement, and love mean the world to me. I don't know how I got so lucky.

Lastly, thank you, dear readers. I promise there are many more great books to come from me- and perhaps from you as well.

Notes

Allow me a brief disclaimer: Much of this book constitutes my own opinions on a very subjective topic. In that sense I do not pretend that it is purely academic, requiring the methodology of a research paper or statistical analysis. That does not discredit the ideas presented- by no means- which are based on sound reason, my own experience and the experience of other professionals, and from looking at what has and has not performed well in the literary world. It simply means that my purpose in creating this section of the book, which most of you will likely skip (which is fine), is not to present a formal bibliography of any sort. I merely wish to cite some of my sources in case any of you would like to check on my quotes and claims. The views and opinions expressed in the text are not without foundation.

Chapter 1

Works Cited:

Clerk, N. W. (Pseud. for C. S. Lewis.) *A Grief Observed.* United Kingdom: Faber and Faber, 1961. Print.

Friedman, Milton. *Capitalism and Freedom.* Chicago: University of Chicago, 1962. Print.

Fulkerson, W.A. *Starfall.* Los Angeles: Createspace, 2013. Print.

Fulkerson, W.A. *The Weathermen.* San Diego: Perennial Press, 2016 (projected). Print.

Hawthorne, Nathaniel. *The Scarlet Letter*. Boston: Ticknor, Reed, and Fields, 1850. Print.

Marx, Karl, and Friedrich Engels. *Communistischer Arbeiterbildungsverein (Eng. - The Communist Manifesto)*. London: Workers' Educational Association, 1848. Print.

McCaffrey, Anne. *The Dolphins of Pern*. New York: Ballantine, 1994. Print.

McCaffrey, Anne. *Dragonquest*. New York: Ballantine, 1979. Print.

McCaffrey, Anne. *Dragonflight*. New York: Ballantine, 1978. Print.

McCarthy, Cormac. *The Road*. New York: Alfred A. Knopf, 2006. Print.

Rowling, J. K. *Harry Potter*. London: Bloomsbury, 1997. Print.

Shelley, Mary Wollstonecraft. *Frankenstein, Or, The Modern Prometheus*. London: Lackington, Hughs, Harding, Mavor, and Jones, 1818. Print.

Tolkien, J. R. R. *The Lord of the Rings*. London: Allen & Unwin, 1954. Print.

Vonnegut, Kurt. *Slaughterhouse-five: Or, The Children's Crusade, a Duty-dance with Death*. New York: Delacorte, 1969. Print.

Claims Supported:

1- In this chapter I state that **Creative Writing is taught very poorly**. This is not merely my opinion, but the opinion of many others as well. Consider, for example, an article ("Show or Tell") by Louis Menand in the June 8, 2009 Issue of *The New Yorker*. In the article, Menand exposes the spectacular failure of even the most well-renowned creative writing programs for creating talented writers. He quotes such writers, industry experts, and critics as Allen Tate, Verlin Cassill, Mark McGurl and others. A Spokesperson for

The University of Iowa's Writing Workshop is also quoted, saying "...writing cannot be taught." That writing "cannot be taught" is a sentiment I wholeheartedly disagree with, but it is instructive to point out that some of our nation's top writing instructors believe it.

There are a number of possible sources not listed here to point the interested reader to further back up my claim, but consider by way of corroboration these few others: Jonathan Morrow (of *Copyblogger: Content Marketing Mastery*), for example, writes: "I think most good writers listen to the way English teachers want them to write and think, 'This isn't real. It has no feeling, no distinctiveness, no oomph. You're the only person in the world who would willingly read it. Everyone else would rather chew off their own eyelids than read more than three pages of this boring crap.' And they're right."

In an October 24, 2013 article in Forbes magazine entitled, "A Key Reason Why American Students Do Poorly," writer George Leef states that American students have notoriously poor writing skills, in part because their teachers are not themselves good writers. He also references Rita Kramer's 1991 book *Ed School Follies: The Miseducation of American Teachers*, saying that "...our ed schools were giving the country a steady stream of intellectually mediocre teachers who had been steeped in dubious educational theories, but often knew little about the subject matter they were to teach. Since then, an avalanche of criticism has come down on education schools, but the only changes have been cosmetic." There are many, many sources where the interested researcher may find corroboration on this point.

2- I talk about the English poet John Donne, making two claims: One, that **John Donne is one of the greatest handlers of the English language**, and two, that **John Donne's poetry reflects a progression in his own life**. To the first point, I offer the following quotation from the Poetry Foundation: "John Donne's standing as a great English poet, and one of the greatest writers of English prose, is now assured." There will always be some measure of debate regarding questions of "greatest" anything, so admittedly my claim mixes both critical consensus and my own opinion. However, I am not alone in my opinion as it is that of many scholars as well. Dr. David Kelly, Professor of English at the University of Sydney, for instance, writes in his scholarly essay "The Canonization of John Donne" the following: "Donne was canonized in the secular, literary sense... Donne is now installed within that canon for writing this and other 'hymns', this and other poems..."

As to the point that John Donne's poetry reflected some sort of progression in his life, I will concede that it is difficult to empirically prove this with certainty, as most of his work was published posthumously and the exact date of many of his poems- "The Flea," for instance- is not presently known. However, I have heard the same claim made during my years of schooling by instructors. I invite the interested reader to study the timeline of his life, available at such resources as The Poetry Foundation and others, and put it against the changing writing style and common themes of his work. That he did not write the "Holy Sonnets" for instance until the latter part of his life is not in dispute. Merely through our knowledge that his flippant poetry came before these supports my claim, though it is harder to demonstrate the timeline of his so-called "romantic" period.

3- At the end of the chapter, **I quote musician Jon Foreman**. The quote comes from an August 11, 2011 interview between Jon Foreman and Dan MacIntosh of *Songfacts*. The transcript of the interview can be found on *Songfacts'* website.

Chapter 2

Works Cited:

Crichton, Michael. *Airframe*. New York: Alfred Knopf, 1996. Print.

Crichton, Michael. *Sphere*. New York: Alfred Knopf, 1987. Print.

Crichton, Michael. *Jurassic Park*. New York: Alfred Knopf, 1990. Print.

Crichton, Michael. *The Thirteenth Warrior: Formerly Titled Eaters of the Dead*. New York: Alfred Knopf, 1976. Print.

Edison, Tommy. *Can Blind People Draw?* Distributed on YouTube.com: TommyEdisonXP, 2013. Online Video.

Edison, Tommy. *Can People Describe Colors to a Blind Person?* distributed on YouTube.com: TommyEdisonXP, 2014. Online Video.

Edison, Tommy. *Describing Colors as a Blind Person.* Distributed on YouTube.com: TommyEdisonXP, 2012. Online Video.

Edison, Tommy. *How Blind People Dream.* Distributed on YouTube.com: TommyEdisonXP, 2012. Online Video.

Fleming, Ian. *Casino Royale.* London: Jonathan Cape, 1953. Print.

Fleming, Ian. *Dr. No.* London: Jonathan Cape, 1958. Print.

Fleming, Ian. *From Russia, with Love.* London: Jonathan Cape, 1957. Print.

Fleming, Ian. *Goldfinger.* London: Jonathan Cape, 1959. Print.

Fleming, Ian. *You Only Live Twice.* London: Jonathan Cape, 1964. Print.

Fulkerson, W.A. *For Whom the Sun Sings.* San Diego: Perennial Press, 2017 (projected)

Griffin, Merv. *Jeopardy!* NBC, Syndicated. First aired 30 Mar. 1964. Television.

Claims Supported:

4- In this chapter I make the claim that author **Ian Fleming "... is credited as being one of the best-selling fiction writers of all time. Even today, nearly sixty years after his death, he continues to sell books and their film adaptations continue to smash the box office every time."** By way of corroboration, consider the April 10th, 2011 article appearing in the "Books" section of *The Guardian*, entitled "Ian Fleming and Agatha Christie lead list of UK's top-earning crimewriters." According to the article: "The first crime writers rich list, prepared for the crime drama digital TV channel Alibi, is based on recorded sales, box office returns, license fees and company accounts. It reveals that many dead writers, including Fleming and Christie, live on as flourishing brands. It puts Fleming in first place at more than £100m, with more than 100m copies of the Bond books sold worldwide." Fleming handily beat out every living British crime writer, and all of the dead ones as well. In the US alone, the last four Bond films have earned estimated box office returns of $167m (Casino Royale, 2006), $168m (Quantum of Solace, 2008), $304m (Skyfall, 2012), and $200m (Spectre, 2015). Again, these numbers reflect *only* US box office sales, which is to say nothing of the extremely large international market these films reach, nor the extended distribution after the duration of the films' theatrical releases. The box office estimations here listed come from IMDB.

5- I also state that **Ian Fleming was a British Naval Intelligence Officer and thus, by definition, a spy**. This is a well-established fact that may be substantiated in any number of available biographies on the man, but for the expedient and interested reader, a short biography of his life is available on the website dedicated to his legacy, ianfleming.com, as well as on biography.com. Books should be generally given greater consideration in research, but there is no disagreement in this case and both will and do substantiate my claim.

6- I mention a term in this chapter, **"sub-creation," and I attribute it to author J.R.R. Tolkien.** The term was first coined by Tolkien in a lengthy essay about the nature of fantasy and mythology entitled, "On Fairy Stories." This was originally entitled simply "Fairy Stories" and was written as an oral presentation that Tolkien gave to the University of St. Andrews in 1939. It first appeared in print in 1947 in a collection compiled by his close friend C.S. Lewis, the larger work being named *Essays Presented to Charles Williams.* For the interested reader, the essay may be found inside of *The Tolkien Reader*, published by Del Rey. It bears mentioning that the nuanced literary critic may contest a subtle difference between Tolkien's usage of the term and my own. I will let the reader decide for himself, yet the difference, if one exists, is small.

Chapter 3

Works Cited:

Coben, Harlan. *Six Years*. New York: Dutton, 2013. Print.

Doyle, Arthur Conan. *The Complete Sherlock Holmes*. Garden City, NY: Doubleday, 1930. Print.

Jagger/Richards. *Paint It Black*. The Rolling Stones. Rec. 8 Mar. 1966. Andrew Loog Oldham, 1966. Vinyl Recording

Shakespeare, William. *Othello*. Whitehall Palace, London. 1 Nov. 1604. Performance. First Published 1622, Thomas Walkley, London

Claims Supported:

7- In this chapter I state that **Stephen King is "...one of the highest-selling, highest-paid, largest-reach authors with more film adaptations of his books than just about any other modern writer."** Consider a October 31st, 2014 article by Jane Ciabattari of BBC, which states "...(King) has published more than 50 books, all of them international best sellers... There are now more than 100 films and TV programmes (sic) based on his work, and he shows no signs of slowing down." It follows logically that the author of an excess of 50 international bestselling works is in the upper tier of reach and salary. However, if that is not sufficient, consider a November 9th, 1998 article by Doreen Carvahal entitled "Stephen King Unleashed" which appeared in the *New York Times*, which states: "Simon & Schuster... paid (King) a $2 million advance against profits for each title in a three-book deal plus a share of the profits of more than 50 percent. Since then, Mr. King has expanded the arrangement to include two more books..." I believe the point to be sufficiently made, but without belaboring, it bears mentioning that it is commonly stated that the typical profits share of the average author is around 8% for paperback and 15% for hardcover. 50% is nigh unprecedented, to say nothing of his enormous advances. As far as my claim concerning his film adaptations, I will offer one further piece of evidence: according to Quora, Stephen King has 86 film adaptations of his books and 178 IMDB credits to his name. It states,

"He is probably the most adapted *living* author." Several classical writers have more adaptations than King, which is why in the text I stressed that he leads "modern" writers.

8- The **Stephen King quote** comes from his own book on writing, aptly named, *On Writing*. In the edition I have access to (ISBN-13: 978-0-7434-5596-1), the quote appears on page 161.

Chapter 4

Works Cited:

Card, Orson Scott. *Ender's Game*. New York: Tor, 1985. Print.

Orwell, George. *1984*. London: Harvill Secker, 1949. Print.

Sanderson, Brandon. *Mistborn: The Final Empire*. New York: TOR, 2006. Print.

Shakespeare, William. *Romeo and Juliet*. London: John Danter, 1597. Print.

Claims Supported:

9- In this chapter I mention a few of the many successes and accolades of Orson Scott Card's *Ender's Game*. A few are self-explanatory, such as his winning of the Hugo and Nebula Awards (it says as much on the front cover, and the foundations responsible for granting these distinctions are easily searchable) and its position on the NY Times' Bestsellers List; a few accolades may require explanation. I mention that ***Ender's Game* is constantly making lists of "best" books.** Here are a few examples: In Locus' "Best SF Novels of All-Time" list (compiled in 2012), *Ender's Game* came in at # 2 all-time in a readers' poll. In 1999 Amazon.com asked users to vote for their favorite books of all-time in their Millennium Poll. *Ender's Game* ranked #32 overall. The Modern Library lists *Ender's Game* as #59 on its readers' list of best 100 novels. Keep in mind that the last two lists mentioned are not restricted to the Sci-Fi genre, but are out of all fiction. In 2011 NPR's readers' poll placed *Ender's*

Game at #3 on a list of top 100 sci-fi/fantasy books. The book appears so many times and with such frequency that it is tiresome and perhaps impossible to exhaust the instances of this book appearing on "best" lists.

10- In this chapter I tell the story of Michelangelo sculpting *David*. **There are two claims I would like to support- first, the story of the carving itself, second, the claim that *David* is "arguably the most magnificent piece of art that man has ever created."** The story itself, as I admit in the text, may be apocryphal. I have heard it from other sources, but not in a manner that I can confidently substantiate it or call it concrete truth. However, most of the story *is* grounded in concrete truth. According to Accademia.org, the official website for the museum that houses *David*, "Michelangelo was asked by the consuls of the Board to complete an unfinished project begun in 1464 by Agostino di Duccio and later carried on by Antonio Rossellino in 1475. Both sculptors had in the end rejected an enormous block of marble due to the presence of too many '*taroli*', or imperfections, which may have threatened the stability of such a huge statue. This block of marble of exceptional dimensions remained therefore neglected for 25 years, lying within the courtyard of the Opera del Duomo... It is known from archive documents that Michelangelo worked at the statue in utmost secrecy, hiding his masterpiece in the making up until January 1504. Since he worked in the open courtyard, when it rained he worked soaked. Maybe from this he got his inspiration for his method of work: it is said he created a wax model of his design, and submerged it in water. As he worked, he would let the level of the water drop, and using different chisels, sculpted what he could see emerging. He slept sporadically, and when he did he slept with his clothes and even in his boots still on, and rarely ate, as his biographer Ascanio Condivi reports." Given his known eccentricities and the amount of time it took him to complete the work (from 1501-1504), it seems to me entirely possible that the supposed "sto lavorando" conversation took place, but as far as I am aware, this last bit is a guess, if a romantic guess.

As to the claim that *David* is arguably "the most magnificent piece of art that man has ever created," it must remain an opinion, though I wish to tell you that standing in the statue's presence literally took my breath away and quieted me from speaking. I cannot say that *David* is objectively the most magnificent artwork, but I do wish to support that others feel the same way. Consider Vasari's description: "When all was finished, it cannot be denied that this work has carried off the palm from all other statues, modern or ancient, Greek or Latin; no other artwork is equal to it in any respect, with such just proportion, beauty and excellence did Michelagnolo finish it."

11- When speaking of the incredible talent of Michelangelo, I make the claim **"he would pick a side and chisel straight forward until it was done,"** which is to say that he did not work in the same manner as other sculptors, but rather worked from one side only (instead of in the round). This is substantiated by many sources, the most prominent of course being Michelangelo's contemporary biographer Georgio Vasari, who, in his work *Lives of the Artists*, describes Michelangelo's process. He tells us that Michelangelo would create a wax cast of the statue to be carved, submerge it in water, and then emerge it, watching which parts became prominent first and how the water ran off the emerging figure. He then was able to attack the stone in the same manner- from one side, as if the excess stone was falling away and a statue was emerging.

I myself have seen many pieces of Michelangelo's work in person, including Michelangelo's so-called "prisoners." These "prisoners" are unfinished works from which we get to see a glimpse of how the master worked. It is apparent that he attacked only one side and worked into the stone, as I claimed, but my word is not the one you should or need to give credence to- the *Galleria dell'Accademia* in Florence, Italy, which houses these prisoners, makes the same claim. The most accessible manner of checking my claim is by checking their website, academia.org, which states the following: "Unlike most sculptors, who prepared a plaster cast model and then marked up their block of marble to know where to chip, Michelangelo mostly worked free hand, starting from the front and working back."

12- **I include a "Japanese Proverb" in this chapter**. The strange thing is, as I sought to substantiate this very commonly quoted and regurgitated quotation, I could find no solid evidence of this sentence originating in Japan, or of it being a traditional proverb at all. Please do not misunderstand- I have found hundreds of occasions wherein the quote is *claimed* to be a "Japanese Proverb," but as of yet I have been unable to find a single scholarly work or serious publication that substantiates this claim. A friend of mine who speaks Japanese helped me look into this, and oddly enough when the quote is searched online in Japanese, it is said to be an *American* Proverb, with English translations listed next to the quotation. The oldest substantial, possible source that I could find comes from Sochiro Honda (the founder of Honda) who once said "Action without philosophy is a lethal weapon and philosophy without action is worthless," though I have also found individuals who believe the quotation to have come from Confucius' writings on learning. As I speak neither Japanese nor Chinese, deep research is difficult, so at this point it remains possible, though doubtable, that this is a traditional Japanese Proverb, though perhaps it came from Mr. Honda (who may have been paraphrasing the original, however), which would technically make it a proverb from Japan, though a modern one. I have left the quotation in the text because the origin is not important to the argument presented.

13- **I include a Henry David Thoreau quote in this chapter**. It comes from the "Conclusion" section of his famous book *Walden*.

Chapter 5

Works Cited:

LaBeouf, Shia, Ronkko & Turner in collaboration with Central Saint Martins BA Fine Art 2015 students. *#Introductions*. Distributed on Vimeo.com: LaBeouf, Ronkko & Turner, 2015. Online Video.

Stack, Levi. *The Magic Trick*. Vol. 2. Createspace, 2014. Print. The Card Game.

Stack, Levi. *The Silent Deal*. Vol. 1. Createspace, 2013. Print. The Card Game.

Tharp, Twyla, and Mark Reiter. *The Creative Habit: Learn It and Use It for Life: A Practical Guide*. New York: Simon & Schuster, 2003. Print.

Claims Supported:

14- I was attending Book Expo America 2014, held at the Javits center in New York, when I heard **John Grisham talk about his experience coming into work early to write**.

15- **The Samuel Johnson quote** comes from chapter 13 of his work *The History of Rasselas, Prince of Abissinia*.

16- **The L'Amour quote** about being able to write in the "middle of Sunset Boulevard" can be found in the "About the Author" section of most of his books (particularly the paperbacks. I found it in "Buckskin Run, ISBN: 0-553-20606-0), where it is attributed to him. He makes similar statements in his memoir *Education of a Wandering Man*.

17- In this chapter I mention that **sometimes in the course of my workflow I find it necessary to nap for a few minutes to let my mind organize what I have been thinking about**, so that I can then write better when I wake up. The cognitive benefits of napping have been studied greatly, and I will support my claim that the occasional nap helps me write better by citing a study by Catherine E. Milner and Kimberly A. Kote which appeared in the June 2009 issue of the *Journal of Sleep Research*, titled "Benefits of Napping in Healthy Adults." According to the article: "...even for individuals who generally get the sleep they need on a nightly basis, napping may lead to considerable benefits in terms of mood, alertness, and cognitive performance... Benefits of napping for waking performance have been confirmed by many researchers... It is particularly beneficial to performance on tasks, such as addition, logical reasoning, reaction time, and symbol recognition."

18- If you'll excuse the obvious hyperbole of the phrase "four hundred million times," I state in this chapter that **writers are more likely to be alcoholics** than most individuals. This is confirmed by a number of sources, but the study that I will use as support comes from the May 1996 issue of the *British Journal of Psychiatry*, titled "Verbal Creativity, depression and alcoholism. An investigation of one hundred American and British writers." From the abstract: "An earlier study of 291 world famous men had shown that only visual artists and creative writers were characterised (sic), in comparison with the general population, by a much higher prevalence of pathological personality traits and alcoholism. Depressive disorders, but not any other psychiatric conditions, had afflicted writers almost twice as often as men with other high creative achievements. The present investigation was undertaken to confirm these findings in a larger and more comprehensive series of writers, and to discover causal factors for confirmed high prevalences of affective conditions and alcoholism in writers." From the Results section of the Abstract: "A high prevalence in writers of affective conditions and of alcoholism was confirmed."

19- I mention in this chapter that **Aaron Sorkin used cocaine as part of his process, and it almost ruined his life.** Stories of his arrests and treatments were well-publicized at the time, but I will provide a few pieces of evidence here. First, consider a November 15th, 2014 interview with Aaron Sorkin conducted by Jane Mulkerrins and appearing in *Independent UK*. According to the article, "Through the Nineties, Sorkin battled drug addiction." Sorkin's own words, appearing in the same article, prove the point that I make in the text better than any other source. He says, "With cocaine, you always feel like you're a rock star, and everything you're writing is fantastic. When I got clean I was terrified of writing. I didn't think I could do it at all." Consider, also, an October 28th, 2001 article by Peter de Jonge titled "Aaron Sorkin Works His Way Through the Crisis," which appeared in the *New York Times*. According to the article, "Both writing and freebasing have proved devastatingly addictive to Sorkin." It also lists an account of at least one of his arrests, saying, "...the network's decision to accommodate Sorkin was a $10 million act of largess, proffered to a man who barely four months before had been arrested at the Burbank airport with a carry-on bag containing marijuana, hallucinogenic mushrooms and crack cocaine. And Sorkin, who was in rehab six years before, admitted that this was not the first time he had fallen off the wagon."

Chapter 6

Works Cited:

Gaiman, Neil. *American Gods: A Novel.* New York: W. Morrow, 2001. Print.

Gaiman, Neil. *Neverwhere.* London: BBC Books, 1996. Print.

Gaiman, Neil. *Stardust.* New York: Avon, 1999. Print.

Claims Supported:

20- **The Neil Gaiman quote** in this chapter comes from Gaiman's '8 Rules of Writing,' appearing in a February 19th, 2010 article on *The Guardian*'s website titled, interestingly enough, "Ten Rules for Writing Fiction." The initial list given is ten rules, but later in the article other prominent authors were asked for their own rules, not all of whom gave ten. Gaiman's full list, for those who are interested, was as follows: "**1** Write. **2** Put one word after another. Find the right word, put it down. **3** Finish what you're writing. Whatever you have to do to finish it, finish it. **4** Put it aside. Read it pretending you've never read it before. Show it to friends whose opinion you respect and who like the kind of thing that this is. **5** Remember: when people tell you something's wrong or doesn't work for them, they are almost always right. When they tell you exactly what they think is wrong and how to fix it, they are almost always wrong. **6** Fix it. Remember that, sooner or later, before it ever reaches perfection, you will have to let it go and move on and start to write the next thing. Perfection is like chasing the horizon. Keep moving. **7** Laugh at your own jokes. **8** The main rule of writing is that if you do it with enough assurance and confidence, you're allowed to do whatever you like. (That may be a rule for life as well as for writing. But it's definitely true for writing.) So write your story as it needs to be written. Write it honestly, and tell it as best you can. I'm not sure that there are any other rules. Not ones that matter."

21- In this chapter, I make the claim that **people are bad at knowing what they will like and good at knowing what they**

don't, based off of what I was taught during my Market Research training at the University of Southern California. This truism may be substantiated in a number of ways, but the simplest is to posit that people understand much better how they feel now than they are at predicting how they will feel in the future. *New York Times* journalist Jon Gertner writes about this phenomenon in his September 7th, 2003 article titled "The Futile Pursuit of Happiness," in which he states, "...when it comes to predicting how you will feel in the future, you are most likely wrong." He's drawing off of the research of Harvard Psychology professor Daniel Gilbert, Univ. of Virginia Psychologist Tim Wilson, Carnegie-Mellon Economist George Loewenstein, and Psychologist/Economic Nobel Laureate Daniel Kahneman of Princeton. Additionally, in an interview concerning his book on the subject, *Stumbling on Happiness*, Daniel Gilbert told Random House the following: "People make mistakes when they try to predict what will make them happy in the future – a process Tim Wilson and I have called 'affective forecasting.'" This relates to my claim because of the advance reading process. Readers are good at knowing what's bad because it's right in front of them. They're bad at making suggestions because in doing so they are making an affective forecast, a thing for which humans are not well-suited.

Chapter 7

Works Cited:

Back to the Future. Dir. Robert Zemeckis. Prod. Steven Spielberg. By Robert Zemeckis and Bob Gale. Perf. Michael J. Fox and Christopher Lloyd. Universal, 1985. Film.

Gangs of New York. Dir. Martin. Scorsese. By Jay Cocks, Steve Zaillian, and Kenneth Lonergan. Perf. Leonardo DiCaprio, Cameron Diaz, Daniel Day-Lewis. Miramax, 2002. Film.

Hemingway, Ernest. *The Sun Also Rises*. New York: Scribner's, 1926. Print.

The Last of the Mohicans. Dir. Michael Mann. Prod. Michael Mann. By Michael Mann and Christopher Crowe. Perf. Daniel Day-Lewis, Madeleine Stowe, and Jodhi May. 20th Century Fox, 1992. Film.

Lewis, C. S. *Surprised by joy: The shape of my early life.* London: Geoffrey Bles. 1955. Print.

Lincoln. Dir. Steven Spielberg. By Tony Kushner. Perf. Daniel Day-Lewis, Sally Field. Dreamworks SKG, Twentieth Century Fox Film Corporation, Reliance Entertainment, 2012. Film.

My Left Foot: The Story of Christy Brown. Dir. Jim Sheridan. By Shane Connaughton and Jim Sheridan. Perf. Daniel Day-Lewis. Ferndale Films, 1989. Film.

There Will Be Blood. Dir. Paul Thomas Anderson. By Paul Thomas Anderson. Prod. Paul Thomas Anderson, Joanne Sellar, and Daniel Lupi. Perf. Daniel Day-Lewis, Paul Dano, Ciarán Hinds, and Dillon Freasier. Paramount Vantage, 2007. Film.

Claims Supported:

22- In this chapter I make the claim that **Ernest Hemingway personally took part in the festival of San Fermin, ran with the bulls, and that his visits are so famous that local pubs and businesses in Pamplona bear his name.** These facts are well-known. Consider the following excerpts from the Huffington Post article "Pursuing Hemingway in Pamplona" by Brooke Self, originally published August 7th, 2012: "He's enshrined here. In more than one location you can find him in bronze. In this Spanish city and traditionally Catholic country, I'm not referring to the Crucifix, or even the co-patron San Fermin, but American author Ernest Hemingway... Hemingway was notoriously an aficionado of bullfights, visiting Pamplona a total of 10 times throughout his life to attend the bullfights and Fiesta of San Fermines... It's no wonder local businesses do all they can to incorporate his name; it's used as a marketing tool throughout the region. My favorite, the 'Panuelico de Hemingway,' a shop found on Estafeta Street, in English it means 'the little handkerchief of Hemingway.'"

I personally have visited Pamplona during San Fermin and have run with the bulls myself, and I can attest that mentions of Hemingway are common. There is an article posted on Sanfermin.com entitled "Did Hemingway Ever Take Part In the Running of the Bulls?" The short answer is yes. The site boasts a picture of Hemingway participating in the event in 1927. The original image currently resides in the John F. Kennedy Library and Museum in Boston, MA, USA, in the Ernest Hemingway Photograph Collection. Additionally, we know from Jose Maria's book *Historia de los Sanfermines* that Hemingway participated.

23- I state that **Daniel Day-Lewis is the only man to have ever won the Oscar for Best Actor on three separate occasions.** The event was widely covered. See *BBC*'s February 25th, 2013 article "Daniel Day-Lewis Makes Oscar History with Third Award," in which the author writes, "Daniel Day-Lewis... the only person to win an Oscar in the best actor category on three occasions." See also *NY Daily News'* article from the same date, entitled "Oscars 2013: Daniel Day-Lewis Becomes Most Decorated Male Actor in Oscars History With Third Best Actor Award for 'Lincoln.'" Many such corroborations exist.

24- I mention many of **Daniel Day-Lewis' awards and accomplishments.** In order to save space in this increasingly lengthy notes section, I will simply refer the reader to Mr. Day-Lewis' "Awards" page on IMDB if you would like to see them in full, though many news articles are available to source my claim as well.

25- I state that **Daniel Day-Lewis was knighted.** I refer the interested reader to two articles, both published on November 14th, 2014. The first, a *UK Daily Mail* story by Ruth Styles, is titled, "Arise Sir Daniel Day-Lewis! Oscar-winning actor is knighted by the Duke of Cambridge in glitzy ceremony in Buckingham Palace." The second, appearing in the *UK Telegraph*, is titled "Daniel Day-Lewis Knighted by the Duke of Cambridge."

26- **The definition for Method Acting** comes from Dictionary.com

27- I mention **two occasions of Daniel Day-Lewis' extreme method acting.** According to the *New York Times*, in an October

31st, 2012 article by Charles McGrath, entitled, "Abe Lincoln as You've Never Heard Him, Daniel Day-Lewis on Playing Abraham Lincoln," we learn the following: "For 'The Last of the Mohicans' he taught himself to build a canoe, shoot a flintlock and trap and skin animals. For the opening scene of 'My Left Foot,' about Christy Brown, an artist with cerebral palsy, he taught himself to put a record on a turntable with his toes; he also insisted on remaining in a wheelchair between takes and being fed by the crew. He learned to box, naturally, for 'The Boxer,' in which he played a prizefighter and former member of the Irish Republican Army and in the process broke his nose and damaged his back. To play the gang leader Bill the Butcher in 'Gangs of New York,' he took butchering lessons, and to play Abraham Lincoln he half-convinced himself that he was Abraham Lincoln."

28- When I refer to being trained by **some of the best instructors in the United States**, I am referring to Red and Black belt holder and former World Jiu Jitsu Champion Fabio Santos, advanced rank black belt Alex Brandao, and advanced rank black belt (and Valet Tudo Champion) Rey Diogo. There will be little to no argument in the martial arts community calling Fabio Santos one of the best instructors in the country. Very few ever attain his rank.

29- I state that **Tom Clancy was unable to serve in the military** so he wrote about it instead. His official (and Facebook verified) Facebook account states as much, stating on a November 11th, 2015 post "Though unable to serve in the U.S. military, Tom Clancy has the Navy to thank for launching his literary career." The fact is well-known that his eyesight kept him out of the service. *Lifetime* (UK) posted an obituary in honor of Tom Clancy after his death on October 1st, 2013. The article begins with the words, "Unable to pass the required eye exam, Clancy's boyhood dreams of serving in the US military were transferred onto his literary ambitions."

30- The **Vonnegut Quote** appeared in the 1977 edition of the *Paris Review*, "The Art of Fiction No. 64"

Chapter 8

Works Cited:

Maltz, Maxwell, M.D., F.I.C.S. *Psycho-cybernetics*. New York: Simon and Schuster, 1960. Print.

Sorkin, Aaron. *The West Wing*. NBC. First Aired 22 Sept. 1999. Dist. Warner Brothers Television. Perf. Martin Sheen, Rob Lowe, Allison Janey, Dule Hill. Television.

Claims Supported:

31- This chapter is a little different than the others as it contains a large amount of verifiable fact. Rather than sourcing every single instance of statements such as 'the psychoanalytic perspective views man in three parts, the id, the ego, and the superego' (the notes section of this book would be as long as the chapter itself, easily, if I were to do this) I will instead provide support for the less objective claims. My aim for this section of notes is to demonstrate that I am not alone in the claims that I make throughout the book. Statements such as "creative writing is taught poorly" can sound dubious when not backed up by scholarly agreement, and so I provide it. All of that to say, if the interested reader would like to check my objective reporting of psychological facts presented in this chapter (those that are not already sourced inside the chapter itself), he is free to read an introductory Psychology textbook.

32- **Soft Science**, according to Dictionary.com: "any of the specialized fields or disciplines, as psychology, sociology, anthropology, or political science, that interpret human behavior, institutions, society, etc., on the basis of scientific investigations for which it may be difficult to establish strictly measurable criteria. Compare hard science."

33- I make the claim in this chapter that **Psychology often has an undue bias on the abnormal mind.** Consider the words of clinical Psychologist Dr. Henry Cloud in his 2011 book, *The Law of Happiness*: "A number of years ago, Martin Seligman (then president of the American Psychological Association) and others championed the message that while psychology had made great strides in its studies on the "negative" side of life – such as depression, trauma, anxiety – it had spent relatively little time studying the "up" side of life. Topics such as happiness, well-being, strengths, etc., had not gained the same amount of attention, especially from scientific research."

34- I state that **bank tellers are trained how to spot counterfeits** by thoroughly understanding a genuine bill, not from knowing various kinds of counterfeits. This fact is found all over the place and is a particular favorite of people discussing faith topics- a trend likely started by Walter Martin in his book *Kingdom of the Cults*, in 1965, which relates the following in its first chapter: "The American Banking Association has a training program that exemplifies this aim of the author. Each year it sends hundreds of bank tellers to Washington in order to teach them to detect counterfeit money, which is a great source of a loss of revenue to the Treasury Department. It is most interesting that during the entire two-week training program, no teller touches counterfeit money. Only the original passes through his hands. The reason for this is that the American Banking Association is convinced that if a man is thoroughly familiar with the original, he will not be deceived by the counterfeit bill, no matter how much like the original it seems." Consider also author Tim Challies, whose blog chronicles his search into whether or not this claim is true (he found that it was, after speaking with a treasury expert). If the interested reader wants to triple check this claim, he is free to call a bank.

35- I state that **the famous quotation attributed to Freud is actually not something Freud likely said**. The first occurrence of this quotation in print appears to be a 1950 article (over a decade after Freud's death) in *Psychiatry* by Allen Wheelis, but he does not source the claim, simply calling the quotation "famous," despite the fact that it had never been printed in English before. I point the interested reader to quoteinvestigator.com, which is a wonderful first place to look for questions of this sort. The site has a great article chronicling why the cigar statement is apocryphal.

Chapter 9

Works Cited:

Children of Men. Dir. Alfonso Cuarón, Mark Fergus, and Hawk Ostby. By Alfonso Cuarón, Timothy J. Sexton, and David Arata. Perf. Julianne Moore, Clive Owen, Chiwetel Ejiofor. Universal Pictures, 2006. Film.

Collins, Suzanne. *The Hunger Games.* New York: Scholastic, 2008-2010. Print.

Dixon, Franklin W. *The Secret of Wildcat Swamp.* New York: Grosset & Dunlap, 1952. Print.

Fulkerson, W.A. *Starfall.* Los Angeles: Createspace, 2013. Print.

Fulkerson, W.A. *The Weathermen.* San Diego: Perennial Press, 2016 (projected). Print.

Fitzgerald, F. Scott. *The Beautiful and the Damned.* New York: Scribner's, 1922. Print.

Huxley, Aldous. *Brave New World.* London: Chatto & Windus, 1932. Print.

Lewis, C. S. *The Chronicles of Narnia.* New York: HarperCollins, 1950-1956. Print.

Melville, Herman. *Moby-Dick.* London: Richard Bentley, 1851. Print.

Rothfuss, Patrick. *The Name of the Wind.* Vol. 1. New York: DAW, 2007. Print. The Kingkiller Chronicle.

Sanderson, Brandon. *Mistborn: The Final Empire.* New York: TOR, 2006. Print.

Tolkien, J. R. R. *The Hobbit.* London: Allen and Unwin, 1937. Print.

Tolkien, J. R. R. *The Lord of the Rings*. London: Allen and Unwin, 1954-1955. Print.

White, T. H. *The Once and Future King*. Glasgow: Collins, 1958. Print.

Zafón, Carlos Ruiz. *The Shadow of the Wind (orig. La Sombra Del Viento)*. Barcelona: Planeta, 2001. Print.

Claims Supported:

36- The **Rothfuss quote** comes from an interview conducted by *Fictional Ferrets* during the 2013 Oklahoma Writers' Federation, Inc. conference.

37- The **10% rule** comes from the same interview mentioned above. The full quote is: "Rule of thumb: 10 percent of what you know should be in your story. For me, it's about 4 percent."

Chapter 10

Works Cited:

Card, Orson Scott. *Magic Street*. New York: Del Rey/Ballantine, 2005. Print.

L'Amour, Louis. *Education of a Wandering Man: A Memoir*. New York: Bantam, 1989. Print.

Shakespeare, William. *A Midsummer Night's Dream (orig. A Midsommer Nights Dreame)*. London: Thomas Fisher, 1600. Print.

Stockett, Kathryn. *The Help*. New York: Berkeley, 2009. Print.

Claims Supported:

38- The **C.S. Lewis quote** comes from his letter to one Joan Kiln of Oxford, written the 26th of June, 1956. A copy of the letter in question, containing the quotation, may be found in the book, "C.S.

Lewis' Letters to Children" (Scribner).

39- The inspiration for the phrase "**You only understand drunkenness when you're sober**" comes from a C.S. Lewis quote that frankly may or may not be relevant to the point raised in the text. However, I happen to think the quotation is brilliant, and I will list it here for those of you reading the notations. It comes from his book *Mere Christianity*. "When a man is getting better he understands more and more clearly the evil that is still left in him. When a man is getting worse he understands his own badness less and less. A moderately bad man knows he is not very good: a thoroughly bad man thinks he is all right. This is common sense, really. You understand sleep when you are awake, not while you are sleeping. You can see mistakes in arithmetic when your mind is working properly: while you are making them you cannot see them. You can understand the nature of drunkenness when you are sober, not when you are drunk. Good people know about both good and evil: bad people do not know about either." Sometimes we have to step outside of a thing to understand it.

40- In this chapter I make the claim that **learning an additional language will change the way you think,** as well as helping you understand your own tongue better. One recent study, published in *Psychological Science* on April 26th, 2015, led by researcher Athanasopoulos P. studied English/German bilinguals and their mono-tongued counterparts. From the abstract: "These findings show that language effects on cognition are context-bound and transient, revealing unprecedented levels of malleability in human cognition." An Emory University cognitive scientist Phillip Wolff, says of the study (to which he was not connected) "If you're a bilingual speaker, you're able to entertain different perspectives and go back and forth." Consider also, the following quotation put forth by the *Hawai'i Counsel on Language Planning and Policy* and the *English As A Second Language Department at the University of Hawai'i at Manoa*: "Contrary to the idea that two languages confuse people, there is evidence that well-developed bilingualism actually enhances one's 'cognitive flexibility' -- that is, bilingual people (including children) are better able to see things from two or more perspectives and to understand how other people think. (Hakuta, 1986). Bilinguals also have better auditory language skills (i.e., they can discriminate sounds of a language more finely) than monolinguals, and they mature earlier than mono-linguals in terms of linguistic abstraction (i.e., ability to think and talk about language). (Albert and Obler, 1978, cited in Cummins, 1994)."

41- When talking about **the Ernest Hemingway "six word story," I mention that the often-repeated story isn't true**. The particular six word story we are concerned with has existed, in some form, since at least 1917 (an article in *The Editor* by William R. Kane suggests "Little Shoes, Never Worn" as a good title for a short story about a mother losing a baby.) The urban legend's stretch of the truth comes from attributing the story to Hemingway (he didn't write it) and from the events that supposedly surrounded its writing: namely, a bet at lunch where Hemingway awed other writers. Frederick A. Wright debunks the myth in his scholarly article, "The Short Story Just Got Shorter: Hemingway, Narrative, and the Six-Word Urban Legend," first published online on May 9th, 2012, then later appearing in *The Journal of Popular Culture*, in volume 47, issue 2, pages 327-340, April 2014. The source for the erroneous legend appears to be Peter Miller, who included the story in his 1991 book, "Get Published! Get Produced!: A Literary Agent's Tips on How to Sell Your Writing." He fails to substantiate the story, leading many to believe, in light of the evidence, that he made it up.

Chapter 11

Works Cited:

Gaiman, Neil. *Neverwhere*. London: BBC Books, 1996. Print.

Kipling, Rudyard. *The Jungle Book*. London: Macmillin, 1894. Print.

Kipling, Rudyard. *Just so Stories*. London: Macmillin, 1902. Print.

Kipling, Rudyard. *Kim*. London: Macmillin, 1901. Print.

Moore, Alan, and Dave Gibbons. *Watchmen*. New York: DC Comics, 1987. Print.

Rorschach, Hermann. *Psychodiagnostik*. Bern: Ernst Bircher, 1921.

Print.

Unknown. *The Epic of Gilgamesh: An English Version with an Introd.* Trans. N. K. Sandars. Harmondsworth, Middlesex: Penguin, 1972. Print. (The original was written perhaps as long as six thousand years ago. As such, knowing the precise date and individual responsible for "first printing" is simply impossible. Tablets with pieces of the work inscribed upon them have been found dating back more than four thousand years. Some claim that a historical Gilgamesh was the originator of the work, but this cannot be adequately substantiated to say for certain.)

Claims Supported:

42- From the *Oxford English Dictionary*: **Inspiration**: n. 1. The action of blowing on or into. 2. The action, or an act, of breathing in or inhaling; the drawing in of the breath into the lungs.

Chapter 12

Works Cited:

The Adventures of Superman. WOR. Synd. MBS, ABC. New York, 31 Aug. 1942 - 4 Feb. 1949. Perf. Bud Collyer, Joan Alexander, Jackson Beck. Radio.

Bowers, Rick. *Superman versus the Ku Klux Klan: The True Story of How the Iconic Superhero Battled the Men of Hate.* Washington, D.C.: National Geographic, 2012. Print.

Manos, James, Jr. *Dexter.* Showtime. First Aired 1 Oct. 2006. Television.

Claims Supported:

43- The **information on the Conley murder**, as well as the associated quotes and details, come from the following sources:

"Teen Kills Brother, Loves TV Show 'Dexter': Life Imitating

Art?" by Michael Mendelsohn, appearing online at ABC News, March 18, 2011.

"Teen Who Strangled Brother Gets Life In Prison: he said he wanted to be like the fictional TV serial killer Dexter" by AP contributor Charles Wilson, last updated October 15th, 2010, appearing online at NBC News.

"Andrew Conley, 'Dexter' Admirer, Has Life Sentence for Murder Upheld by Ind. Court" by *Crimesider* Staff, appearing online at CBS News, August 1st, 2012.

44- I claim that the Conley murder is tragically not unique, that **other murderers have been inspired to kill by the television show** *Dexter*. Here are a few sources to back up that claim:

"The 'Dexter' Murders: The popular TV series has inspired some very bizarre copycat acts" is a January 18th, 2014 *Psychology Today* article by Katherine Ramsland, Ph.D. It chronicles five *Dexter*-inspired murders besides the one spoken of in the chapter

"Teen Confesses to Killing, Dismembering Girlfriend in Another 'Dexter'-Inspired Murder" by Kristine Marsh of the Media Research Center, appeared online at *CSN News* on October 6th, 2014.

"Teenager Obsessed with TV Killer Dexter Stabbed and Dismembered Girlfriend" is an article appearing in *The Guardian* October 2nd, 2014, by Press Association.

"Murderer Who Was Inspired by Dexter is Given Unlimited Access to Serial Killer TV Show from his Prison Cell" is an article appearing in *UK Daily Mail* on May 6th, 2013, written by Rachel Quigley.

45- The **Thoreau quote** comes from Chapter III. of his book *Walden*, entitled "Reading."